OSCAR®-WINNING

SCREENWRITERS

ON

SCREENWRITING

OSCAR®-WINNING SCREENWRITERS ON SCREENWRITING

THE AWARD-WINNING BEST IN THE BUSINESS DISCUSS THEIR CRAFT

JOEL ENGEL

HYPERION

NEW YORK

Library of Congress Cataloging-in-Publication Data

Engel, Joel.
Oscar-winning screenwriters on screenwriting : the award-winning
best in the business discuss their craft / Joel Engel.
p. cm.
Interviews conducted and edited by Joel Engel to
appear as monologues.
Contents: William Goldman—Robert Benton—Ron Bass—
Michael Blake—John Irving—Tom Schulman—Frank Pierson—
Bo Goldman—Marc Norman—Alan Ball—Stephen Gaghan.
ISBN 0-7868-8690-0
1. Motion picture authorship.   2. Screenwriters—United
States—Interviews.   I. Title.
PN1996 .E57   2002
808.2'3—dc21
2001039699

FIRST EDITION

Designed by Linda Dingler

10   9   8   7   6   5   4   3   2   1

To my aunt and uncle, Beth and Oscar.
We only disagree on movies

Contents

INTRODUCTION 1

WILLIAM GOLDMAN 7

ROBERT BENTON 24

RON BASS 41

MICHAEL BLAKE 63

JOHN IRVING 81

TOM SCHULMAN 97

FRANK PIERSON 114

BO GOLDMAN 132

MARC NORMAN 147

ALAN BALL 164

STEPHEN GAGHAN 184

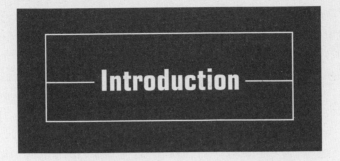

Introduction

THERE'S A JOKE ABOUT THE POLISH STARLET AT A HOL-
lywood party. The punch line is that she goes home
with the screenwriter.

If you can get past the cruel stereotyping you realize
that the joke isn't on Poles; it's on screenwriters. For reasons known best to God, the screenwriter falls somewhere
on the Hollywood food chain between the makeup artist
and the camera operator, both of whose jobs, by the way,
depend on the script written by the screenwriter.

So do the jobs of the producer and director and stars
and everyone else. The DNA of all filmed entertainment
is a script that many of these same people consider little
more than typing. No less than Jack Warner is said to
have once screamed, "I can throw a nickel out the window
right now and hit five screenwriters." Apocryphal or not,
the line remains true in the minds of many who consider
screenwriting to be the thing they'd do themselves if only
they had time. To them, screenwriters are a necessary evil.
Someone has to do the typing.

True, this is more stereotyping—but only a little exaggerated. The disdain for screenwriters shows even in people who should know better: other writers. Notice how often newspaper critics and columnists credit the director for a film's success—and mention the screenwriter only when heaving brickbats (or when the writer is also the director).

Anyone who has ever tried to write a script knows that writing is thinking. "All you do," Gene Fowler once explained, "is stare at a blank sheet of paper until drops of blood form on your forehead." The work of a screenwriter, like the work of a novelist, is to transform imagination into a facsimile of reality by creating characters we care about in stories that engage us. The difference between them is that novels build intimate relationships between readers and authors; authors suggest images that readers "see" on the screen in their brains, images that are unique to them. But screenplays don't really exist until they're made into movies, and in movies, the viewer's relationship is to a thirty-foot screen that flickers with images everyone else sees, too. A successful movie conveys the illusion of not being written at all, but of being created in that moment of viewing.

I will never forget the experience that cemented this notion for me. I was assigned to write a biography of the then recently deceased Gene Roddenberry, the creator of *Star Trek*. Never having been a "Trekkie" and knowing nothing at all about *Star Trek: The Next Generation*, which was then on the air, I attended a symposium sponsored by the Museum of Broadcasting (now called the

Museum of Television and Radio). Onstage were several of the show's primary actors, including Patrick "Captain Picard" Stewart, and its five top writer-producers. A *Next Generation* episode was shown, after which the audience was invited to ask questions of the guests. The first question, directed to Mr. Stewart by a well-dressed man of about forty, was whether the *Enterprise* crew planned to someday revisit the particular planet on which that episode had taken place. Mr. Stewart graciously referred the question to Rick Berman, the show's executive producer (and therefore head writer), and when the question was answered the moderator pointed to another questioner, a young woman. She directed her question to a cast member and asked about the *Star Trek* universe, and again she was referred to one of the writers for an answer. This sequence repeated for the rest of the hour. It became an increasingly funny joke that apparently only those onstage understood. None of the questioners thought to ask the writers where the *Enterprise* was headed next. Their bond was with the actors and the scenery. Of course, you might dismiss these people as science-fiction fans whose connections to reality may be tenuous. But how then do you explain Sally Field's and Jessica Lange's and Sissy Spacek's testifying before Congress in 1984 about the plight of the American farmer, solely because they'd all starred in farm-themed movies that year? Meanwhile, those who'd written the words these actresses spoke in the film weren't within two time zones of the committee hearing.

Well you know what? Writers don't care. They're used to the lack of appreciation and respect. Respect? Writers don't need no stinkin' respect (apologies to B. Traven and John Huston, writers of *Treasure of the Sierre Madre*). They know they have the best job in the world, and no choice in the matter anyway. Even if they wanted to stop writing, they couldn't. Like the priesthood, writing is a calling. That's why those who aren't called to the keyboard can't muster the discipline it takes to hatch a screenplay whose gestation is often longer than that of a human embryo. In fact, a script is very much a baby. You conceive it in an act of love; you cradle it and nurse it and nurture it and shape it and then send it out into the world to succeed. It's your creation, a piece of you. Sex should be so fulfilling.

Some years ago, the cover of an *Esquire* magazine depicted a chimp at a typewriter and asked, "Is anyone in America *not* writing a screenplay?" Personally, I hope not. And everyone who loves movies should hope not. The world needs more writers writing better movies.

To that end, I offer this book. I think of it as a kind of mentor program, providing an intimate experience between you the reader and eleven screenwriters who excel at their craft. (All of them have won Oscars for screenwriting.) They are the people who imagine new worlds and invite everyone else—from the actors whose characters will inhabit those worlds, to the stylists who dress the actors, to us the paying customers—into the darkened theaters where their worlds come alive.

This book is intended for everyone who loves movies, but particularly for aspiring screenwriters in search of information that will help them transform their good ideas into memorable (or at least saleable) screenplays. And thanks to the generosity and insights of the screenwriters interviewed here, every page offers something of use. It was with a sense of awe and respect for their ability to fill blank pages with movies-in-waiting, as well as a deep curiosity, that I asked my questions. They were questions, I think, that civilians would ask of professionals if they had the chance to sit in a room with them and the permission to fire away. Our conversations explored the profession of screenwriting as much as the creative process. And sometimes the answers flowed into far-flung places that seemed only distantly related to screenwriting until I saw how the whole picture fit together.

My previous book on this subject, *Screenwriters on Screenwriting,* was similarly aimed at aspirants. To my surprise, I have seen it on the shelves of some of Hollywood's most prominent citizens and on the coffee tables of ordinary movie fans who have no ambition to write but do have an interest in learning more about their favorite art form. That's a hopeful sign. Everyone should recognize that while bad movies are often made from good scripts, good movies are never made from bad scripts.

As a final introductory note, let me explain that I decided to change the format from *Screenwriters on Screenwriting,* which was done Q&A style. For this book, I wanted to establish a direct connection between the screenwriter and the reader, which meant eliminating myself from the page. To that end I edited the screenwriters' verbal responses to my questions into a form that looks more or less like an essay. But these are not essays; they're monologues. They were spoken, not written, and were edited to maintain the jangled, unpolished, colloquial rhythms of ordinary speech, with all of its fabulous tangents and detours. I let the conversations flow in any direction that seemed interesting, and was nearly always surprised by what I heard. My hope is that, as you read, you will be able to imagine yourself in some dark coffeehouse, listening to accomplished storytellers talk directly to you—as they did to me.

JOEL ENGEL

June 2001

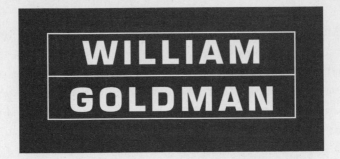

WILLIAM GOLDMAN

Bill Goldman is generally considered the dean of American screen-writers. His opinions are as entertaining as they are honest. We met in his New York penthouse, which looks like a place Noël Coward should have dined, and my first question had to do with *All the President's Men*. How, I asked, was he able to keep up the suspense when everyone already knew the outcome of the story?

In a book you want the reader to turn pages in order to find out what's going to happen. In a movie, you want them to sit there and keep wondering what's going to happen. In both cases, it's the job of the writer to keep them wondering. So what do you do when everyone knows the story you're telling? That was the problem with writing *All the President's Men*. This wasn't a case of re-telling a historical event that had happened a hundred years ago, like the assassination of Lincoln. Watergate had been the news story of the century, and you'd have had to wake the dead to find someone who didn't know what happened or how it turned out.

And in fact I was terrified, because everybody did know the story, and we were all sick of it. I remember I had what I thought was a wonderful opening: a really cornball shot of the Washington Monument, and then an equally cornball shot of the Watergate Complex, and then a shot of the burglars going up to the door and breaking in—and they'd brought the wrong key—which did happen in reality—so they had to go back to Florida to get another key. I thought that was a neat opening, because that was my way of saying to the audience that you don't really know what really happened; you just think you know. But because of length and a bunch of other factors, we just began with the guard at the Watergate seeing the tape.

There were also other, less artistic, considerations that went into the script construction. One of them was the fear of lawsuits. Warner Bros. was terrified of them, terrified that if we strayed from the book that was written by Bob Woodward and Carl Bernstein about how they'd brought down the president, we'd get sued. So we were obliged to stick with the source material, because studios do not like lawsuits, and they especially do not like having to spend X million dollars and then having to wait to release their movie and therefore not get their investment back because of a lawsuit that is delaying distribution. The feeling was that if we stayed exactly with the book, any lawsuits would be weak ones, because the book had been out for a year and no one had sued yet. So we stayed with the book, which meant we essentially went with Woodward and Bernstein, and so their story became the movie—a detective movie.

I think Redford, as one of the producers (with Walter Coblenz), always knew in a crazy way that, even though he and Dustin Hoffman were both terrific, they were miscast. These guys, Woodward and Bernstein, had been unknowns and probably should have been played by unknowns. That would have made the idea of bringing down the president even more astounding.

I'll give you an example: There's a scene in *Misery* where the woman wants the writer to burn his book, and he won't do it, and she says, "Fine, don't do it. I would never want you to do anything that you don't want to do, because I love you and you're wonderful and you're a great writer," and while she's giving that speech she's flicking lighter fluid on his bed where he's lying crippled. The director, Rob Reiner, always wanted to go with an unknown in that part because the character (played by Kathy Bates) was an unknown herself; she was this figure that came out of the blizzard and rescued him and we knew nothing about her. Well, Rob wanted an unknown to play an unknown, just as he wanted a star—Jimmy Caan—in the part of the writer, because the writer was a famous man. The feeling was that if we had Meryl Streep or Glenn Close or any of those wonderful ladies, the audience wouldn't really have believed that she was capable of incinerating Jimmy Caan. Well, in 1990, nobody really knew who Kathy Bates was—at least, not the way they do today. So the writing, the story, the performances, were all helped by the casting.

People often look past this part of filmmaking, but it's important. Redford understood the realities of the movie business, and he knew that *All the President's Men* would never get made with unknowns in the parts. And the reason is that Warner Bros., in my opinion, did not want to make the movie; and I think they only made it to please Redford, because it was something he cared about. And he was such a giant star at the time that, once he was involved, they were obliged to go out and get another star. If they hadn't, if they'd gone with an unknown in the Carl Bernstein part, the movie would have looked unbalanced. As it happened, there were only two stars of sufficient magnitude who could have been cast: Dustin Hoffman and Al Pacino. Well, they went first to Hoffman, and he said yes. So that was that. But I think, ultimately, hewing to the detective story was the only way, because everyone was terrified that the public already knew too much.

What complicated things further were all those horrible names that everyone had to remember. Bob Woodward was a huge help there, helping me to focus on just the story and what was important. The story was the thing. And I have to tell you, as I get older, I think more and more that movies are only story, and if you stay on the story you have a chance to make a good movie. The moment you veer away from the story I think the movie's in trouble. Sure, it may be a hit, but I think it's not going to be very good. That happens, too.

One of the reasons that detective stories tend to work— or at least, they used to work—is that they focus primarily on the story: the unfolding of story through the detective's eyes. *Harper,* based on Ross Macdonald's *The Moving Target,* was a detective story. You follow that guy, Lew

Harper, but he doesn't know everything; he's finding things out along the way. And so that kind of story works well. That kind of storytelling enables the reader, or the viewer, to find out what really happened at the same time that the main character finds it out. Story, story, story.

In my experience—and I hope it's not just my age—there is today less and less attention paid to story. Studio executives, for the most part, don't care to read scripts; they really just want to make the deal. Here's why, I think: Every studio executive knows he's going to get fired. The hottest kid in the business, a guy I've never met, Mike De Luca, was just canned because he had *Thirteen Days* and *Little Nicky* and a Warren Beatty film they may never release, *Town & Country* (released in May of 2001). And I assume that, as brilliant as De Luca's record has been, New Line lost at least a quarter billion on those three—so he's gone. Well, that happens to everybody in this business.

In the long run, De Luca will be fine, because not only do executives know they're going to get fired, they also have a deal in place for when they do. So they don't care about being fired. What they care about is stars and star directors and prolonging their time close to the fire for as long as they can. Everybody wants to stay close to the fire, and it's a terrible thing out there. I think one of the reasons I've survived in this business for more than thirty-five years is that I live in New York, and nobody here cares about the business. In L.A., everybody's in the movie business, and I've seen people turn away from people who were once hot and famous and now aren't, because they don't want to be contaminated with failure. It's hard to write in that kind of atmosphere.

The other thing about that is, I'm nearly seventy. Out there, they don't like people my age, because we're cranky and we're expensive and all of that. I'm very aware that, each time I get a job, it may be my last one. Every time the phone rings, that's terrific.

You see, part of that crankiness is having no patience for the slop that's mostly produced. I think the movies (in 2001) that were up for the Oscars were mostly sloppy stories that could have been taken care of if anyone had cared to. But no one did.

In my opinion the nineties were the worst decade in movie history—and the year 2000 was the worst single year in movie history. To explain that, you have to notice throughout history how talent tended to cluster. The ancient Greek playwrights, the Elizabethan playwrights, and the Russian novelists are examples. Unfortunately, there are also cluster periods when the arts are at a low ebb. And I think we're now in one of those periods—for all the arts, by the way.

You also have to factor in how movie production costs are escalating so badly. How, for example, do you manage to spend $90 million on *Thirteen Days*? That movie was guys sitting around a room, talking. So movie executives are terrified—terrified of costs. And you know what? They should be, because movie attendance keeps going down each year. Sure, the dollar grosses keep going up, but only because they keep raising ticket prices.

Look, *Crouching Tiger, Hidden Dragon* and *Traffic*

both have fabulous stuff in them. The visuals in *Tiger* were wonderful and all that, just marvelous. But when did the maid do all those murders? On her day off? Where were the kid's parents? This girl is flying around on the walls and the roof for ten years and they never said, "No, no, get down off the roof, you're going to get over-excited"? I mean, why doesn't the girl who can fly go back quickly to get the medicine for her dying lover? What's the point of a big fight in the bamboo trees? Hell, they can't fall, they can fly! And I thought it was just horseshit.

In *Traffic,* I hated the Michael Douglas part. Michael Douglas is a brilliant man and a terrific actor, so it wasn't that. It was that the movie was more about Hollywood than about the world it was supposed to be portraying. Here you've got this guy, the drug czar, and the single most important event of his life is to find his daughter, which he manages to do by horseshit—by following her boyfriend to a drug-ridden area. How come the boyfriend never looks around? I thought, Holy shit! I look around every twenty feet when I'm on Forty-second Street.

What irritates me about this stuff is, it's not a big deal to fix it. It's just that nobody cared and nobody bothered and the fact is, when the critic in the *New York Times* says that *Traffic* is a great movie, you want to shoot him, because that kind of thing just gives more license to the people who make movies not to care about the stories they film. They just don't pay attention to story anymore. Maybe because of all the other technologies, they figure that all they have to do is put something that looks good on the screen.

When you see a movie like *Mission: Impossible,* you expect a certain kind of reality, and coherence doesn't matter as much as the ride and the amount of popcorn sold. Not everything does make sense—or has to. But when you're doing *Crouching Tiger,* and this old maid is a villain, it's time to get angry. There's an awful scene in that movie where the two women kick at each other, and I remember thinking that neither of them can hurt each other because of the story; you couldn't have either one of them killing the other or damaging the other, because they're the heroes. I just thought a lot of it was silly.

It really upsets me to say that movies stink now, because I love movies. To see what's happened to American movies, how atrocious they've become, is very, very unsettling and upsetting. It's been way too long since I've heard people talking and talking about a particular movie. The movies I liked best in 2000 were *You Can Count on Me* and *Best in Show.* Those are really special movies, but neither of them is a big Hollywood movie that you can use as a bellwether to say that things are okay.

I mean, how often do we have to have three or four movies coming out within a few weeks of each other, each of them costing at least $70 million—and they all tank. That's what happened recently with a Will Smith movie, and an Adam Sandler movie, and a John Travolta movie. There was absolutely no interest in any of them. And you keep thinking that people are going to finally get it, and they never do, because what happens is that *The Grinch* and *Mission: Impossible II* were the biggest movies of 2000, and both were star driven, so the studios say, "See, stars work," and so they continue to build everything around the stars.

Paul Newman said something really important to me years ago. He said, "I'm not worth anything in a bad movie, and I'm not really worth anything in a movie where I'm miscast. But if I'm cast properly in a quality movie, I think I'm worth more in it than an unknown would be." And I think that's true.

Here's what I do now when I'm offered a script. I ask certain questions, like "Do you need a star?," because that affects how a story is told. I ask, "What rating do you need?" It's not that I really care about the rating per se; it's that I want to know how they see their material, and this is an easy way to figure that out. And then I ask myself whether I can make it work, trying to meld all of these sensibilities and requirements.

When Zanuck ran 20th Century–Fox in the 1960s, he could still say, "Let's make the movie and hope they can sell it." Now the sales people are involved in everything. And that's fine. I'm all for studios making money. A studio has as much right to make money as Bill Gates does. You want to turn out a product that will be pleasing to an audience. The problem is that we don't know how to do that. For example, I have a movie that'll be finished shooting soon, called *Hearts in Atlantis,* and I have no idea what will happen. It's based on a wonderful Stephen King novel, and the shoot has gone marvelously. But what nobody knows is, first, will it cut together, so that it holds as a story? And if it does hold together, will anybody go to see it? Nobody knows anything. I wrote that decades ago, and there's still no one who knows. The week before *Titanic* opened, someone who was involved with it said to me, "If it only does $100 million, we'll be okay." The truth is that you can't tell anything about the box office until you get out there on that Friday.

What's awful is when you have a movie that you like and the people don't go to see it. I remember being told that *The Princess Bride* was the second highest testing movie of its year, so it should have been a blockbuster, right? Well, it wasn't. Not until it got to cassette did it find its audience. It's painful when you look at a movie and think how much you like it, and then see that no one's buying tickets.

In many ways, the audience has changed since I began writing movies. It's my sense that *Butch Cassidy* could not be made today, and would not be made. There's not enough action. I think it would seem slow. Whenever kids see it for the first time I always ask how they liked it. They say it's slow. Of course, these kids are used to MTV. You know, if MTV had originated in the 1930s, you would have seen Fred Astaire dancing for three minutes with the camera far back, and you'd have been able to see him working his magic. What has happened with MTV is that today's performers are essentially studio musicians; they are not bona fide performers. In my day, musical people knew how to sing. But what the hell do you do with guys who can't do much more than strum their guitars and wail? They can't really perform in the sense of an Astaire or Gene Kelly, who trained for years and years to do what they did in front of people. So what you do is, you resort to flash-cutting in order to hide the obvious. Well, the kids like it, and they're the number one market for movie tickets; and at the same time the studios are trying to hire cheap directors for their low-end movies—MTV directors, who don't know about anything other than flash-cutting. That's what we're dealing with.

You know, I never saw a screenplay until I was thirty-three years old. By then I'd written half a dozen novels. That's what I wanted to be, a novelist; I'd never thought about writing movies.

I think you have to face, sooner or later, that screenwriters often write for the screen instead of some other form because of the money. I recently spoke with a young, mildly successful screenwriter who'd just had his first novel published to very good reviews. I asked whether he'd started his second novel yet, and he said, "Why? That was a year in my life, I made ten thousand dollars, I've got a family, and nobody read the book. So why should I write another novel?" In that sense, he was right.

Novelists are alone all the time, and that can get difficult. My wonderful ex-wife remembers that when I was writing novels and not movies, what I missed were the meetings, because there's at least something social about them. Even getting notes from producers and executives is social. But on the other hand, it's probably not healthy to be *just* a screenwriter either; there has to be a balance. Maybe that's just the way my world was constructed, from the time I grew up.

When I was growing up in the 1930s and '40s, movies were a guilty pleasure. Nobody took them seriously. I remember when I first heard of film schools, I wondered why anyone would go to one. Now *everybody* goes to film school, because movies have moved from being silly, lovely, wonderful entertainment, to being the center of our culture. They dominate the world. All the other countries bitch that no one goes to see their movies, they go to see our movies. Occasionally something will break through, but for the most part we dominate the world. So kids today grow up already wanting to be movie people, something that didn't happen when I was a kid.

When I was a kid, you'd walk up to the local theater and pay a dime, and it was magical. We didn't have competing forms of entertainment. We had radio, which was the dominant thing then, and then basically movies came along and began to talk, and suddenly you could have these glamorous and sunny experiences that weren't available to you before.

The other advantage we had then was that we didn't know anything about the stars. We thought of them as actually being their magical personas; we didn't know that they were really neurotic assholes. Now, not only do we know everything about them and their sexual proclivities, we also have TV, music, video games, the Internet. Much of the magic has gone out of entertainment, including and especially the movies. It's as though a kind of world-weary cynicism has infected everything having to do with popular entertainment. I'll give you an interesting and ironic example of that.

Let's take a movie I thought I was going to love called *Three Kings*. Its first sixty-five minutes were magical and fabulous; it was a movie about, well, greed, and it was great; it worked. And then all of a sudden George Clooney says, "We've got to save these Arabs." And I thought, "Where the hell did that idea come from?! You're soldiers of fortune, you're in it for the money." Was that a studio insistence? I'll bet you the farm that it was not the screen-writer's idea—that this stupid idea was not in the script's first draft. I'm sure it wasn't, because the notion put the lie to the whole movie. I was so crushed; if the last forty minutes had been as good as the first sixty-five, it would have been a worldwide blockbuster.

Butch Cassidy and the Sundance Kid, I thought, was a movie that held together. It's a good, solid piece of story-telling. What I did was edit the real-life story with only one, I think, major change. What really happened is that the real Harriman formed a superposse, an all-star team of lawmen, but when Cassidy heard about them he im-mediately ran to South America, and so he and Sundance never actually faced the superposse. Well, even though I was very new to screenwriting at the time, I knew enough to know that Westerns are based on confrontations, and your hero can't run away like that.

So what I had to invent was a way to get them the hell out of America. I invented the superposse chase, in the middle third of the movie. It was simply a plot point to get them out of town. It runs for half an hour and is beautifully directed by George Hill, and it worked! No one ever said, "Well, why are they running away?"

The other thing about that movie was the ending. End-ings are always hard, but this one absolutely worked, and it worked because Butch Cassidy and history gave it to me. It ended, literally, with guns blazing.

There's one last thing that I know to be true about the people who work in Hollywood: Very, very few of us, and this includes performers, dated the cheerleader. And then they became successful and did get the cheerleader—and that's almost worse, in a way. The danger in Hollywood is wanting to stay so close to the fire, as I said earlier. Once you've been hot, you want to always be hot. You want to be told you're wonderful, even when you know you're not. It's dangerous when you hit all of a sudden, and there are people constantly running up to you to tell you that you're a god and they love your hair and oh, where'd you get those fabulous glasses. For a moment, at least, you have magic—and the magic is that you may be able to make them money. The sad thing happens when people begin to believe that they really do have magic. That's when so many careers that started out wonderfully begin to fizzle, because you think, "Well, I'm just so great, it doesn't matter," and then time goes on and you're not wanted and then one day you wake up and find yourself on the outside looking in.

Now, the fact is that I've lasted in the business for more than thirty-five years, and I have absolutely no understanding of why. I basically never think of myself as having particular talent one way or the other, because the minute I do that, things get dangerous. When I deal with young writers, which I like to do, one of the first things on my agenda is to disabuse them of the notion that I know what I'm doing. I don't. I really don't. If I did, everything I write would be terrific, and it isn't.

What I do know is that you don't become a writer because you want to be Jacqueline Susann. You become a
writer because somebody of some quality moved you
when you were a kid and you thought, "Okay, I want to
be Chekhov." And so you decided to be a playwright, but
then when you go into the pit you realize you're never
going to be Chekhov; you're not going to be as good;
you're going to be, in fact, second rate. So right away,
your career can never measure up to your brightest hopes.
Same if you're a novelist; you're not going to be Dostoyevsky. Same with screenwriters; you're not going to be
Ingmar Bergman or Billy Wilder. There's always the sense
that what you're doing is essentially not of great quality,
and that's the sense you have to fight every day. For me,
the hardest thing when I start a project is building up
confidence.

I'm about to start writing a screenplay, one that's based
on a book. What I've been doing is reading and rereading
the source material, and each time I come to something
that seems strong or important, I make a mark in the margin with a different colored pen. By the time I come to do
the screenplay, if there are five or more different marks in
the margin, I'll know that scene or thought is going to be
in the movie. If there's only one mark, I know it won't
be. What all of that is intended to do is to build up confidence; I'm trying to find the spine, the story, so that I
can write it.

Example: The movie *A Bridge Too Far* was a long
movie—three hours—and was intended as such, so the
climaxes therefore came at different times. I was afraid of
that, afraid that I wouldn't understand the storytelling

rhythms. Well, the movie was about the battle of Arnhem, for which the English awarded more Victoria Crosses than for any other battle, so I also knew that no matter how badly I screwed the thing up, I'd have sensational battle scenes to save me. That was my safety net. And then I finally realized what the story was about: It was about the cavalry riding to the rescue—and failing. Well, as it turned out, none of the Victoria Cross pieces made it into the story, but if I'd been told early on that I couldn't use any of them, I really don't know whether I'd have done the movie. I wouldn't have had the confidence.

Anyway, the key is to find the spine, and that's not easy; you have to look and look and look, and it may take months—but once I do, I put a piece of paper on my wall with about twenty-five or thirty words that describe what the movie is about.

I also have to know the ending. I have to know where I'm going. Interestingly, I don't necessarily need to know that in a novel. But novels are longer, and you can take your time getting there, as long as you're amusing yourself along the way. Movies are only 120 pages, with a lot of white space on each page.

Where you enter a scene depends on what element of story that scene has to tell. Example: A teacher says to his class, "Here we see where Wordsworth—" and then the bell rings, and as the class files out a pretty girl comes up and says, "I'm pregnant." Well, the reason nearly every teaching scene in movies goes that way is because you'd die of boredom if you really heard even a stimulating discussion about Wordsworth; there's nothing going on there to look at. Yes, a book can and often does linger with thoughts about Wordsworth, as long as the writing and the thoughts are good. But a movie can't. In a movie, the only reason to have the line about Wordsworth at all is to set the scene, which is really about the pretty, pregnant girl and the teacher. Where you enter and where you exit a scene have everything to do with what just happened and with what's coming next. I am always looking for what connects one scene to the next.

Let's face it, movies are very hard to write. I mean, everything's hard to write, but movies have the added burden of the camera. The camera tells you everything so fast, there's no time to linger. Movies are not about niceties of dialogue. Nice dialogue is better than dumb dialogue, but for the most part the camera's what you're writing for— and it's what the viewer is waiting for. The writer has to be a storyteller through the camera, and that's an odd skill. I guess I must've had it when I started out, because my screenwriting career began when I doctored a movie, then I wrote *Harper,* then I wrote a movie that didn't happen, and then I wrote *Butch Cassidy.* That was within three years of never having seen a screenplay, so I must have had some facility pretty early on, because the truth is that I'm not any better now.

Maybe the most useful thing I ever heard about making movies came from George Roy Hill, who was the best director I've ever worked with. What he told me is what I sometimes pass on to younger writers, especially with movies running way too long these days. George said, "If you can't tell your story in an hour and fifty, you better be David Lean."

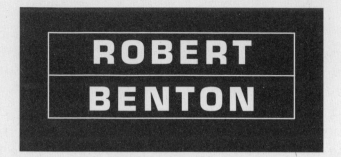

ROBERT BENTON

There are few writer-directors whose films I rush to see. Robert Benton is at the top of that list. His work is made by adults and for adults, and I never feel that the time spent watching was time wasted. The stories he tells are built around endlessly fascinating characters whose worldviews are tinged with cynicism. I don't know why I was so surprised to find that he is a gentle, courtly, courteous man. My first questions seemed obvious: How do you go from never having written a screenplay before, to writing a cinema landmark, *Bonnie and Clyde*? And why?

OKAY, IN THE EARLY SIXTIES I HAD JUST BEEN FIRED FROM my job as the art director of *Esquire* magazine, where I'd been for about seven years, and I couldn't find a job at another magazine—at least not one I'd want to work for, and no advertising agency would hire me. I had just turned thirty and I was dead in the water.

Now let me take a step back: As a child growing up in Texas I had been dyslexic, although no one knew there was such a thing as dyslexia in those days. Consequently,

I was considered both slow and hyperactive at the same time. My father, who was a remarkable man, would come home from work at night and instead of asking me if I had done my homework, which is what most fathers would have done, he would ask if I wanted to go to the movies. He knew that there were two things that could hold my concentration for more than ten minutes at a time. One was drawing and the other was watching movies. So I went to movies a lot (I think my record was seven in one day). I could watch a movie and follow the narrative attentively in a way that wasn't possible with books. When I tried to read I would have to give up after ten minutes and do something else before coming back to it.

We lived in Waxahachie, Texas, a small town not far from Dallas, and when I was in high school I was allowed to go to art classes there. In Dallas there was an "art house" movie theater and I began to see a lot of European films: pictures like *La Symphonie Pastorale, Children of Paradise, The Red Shoes,* and *Rashomon.* Movies like this made a huge impression on me. When I went to the University of Texas I majored in art, but while I was there I became very involved with a girl who was a writer, and so I ended up taking a lot of courses in literature in order to be around her. Fortunately for me the dyslexia had begun to go away by then, but nevertheless I still had to figure out strategies for reading. Try being dyslexic and getting through *The Magic Mountain* in three weeks. In addition, we all went to the movies in those days and movies were all we talked about. And remember the fifties were a pretty desolate period in American filmmaking, so when a picture like *Singin' in the Rain* came out it was a revelation.

I graduated from college and went to New York to go to graduate school at Columbia. I shared an apartment with two other guys, went to Columbia, worked part-time at the law library, and also at night doing pasteups and mechanicals for liquor ads.

After a semester I ran out of money, dropped out of Columbia, and tried to make a living as an illustrator. Needless to say, I had a lot of free time on my hands. In those days I used to hang out in Brentano's, reading books that I could not afford to buy. Actually, I read a good part of Eisenstein's *Film Form* while standing at a table in Brentano's. The other place I used to go all the time was to the Museum of Modern Art to the film showings. I remember that that was where I first saw *Citizen Kane.* Then I went to work as the assistant to Henry Wolf, who was the art director of *Esquire* magazine. Afterward I was drafted and spent two years in El Paso, Texas, going to movies—it wasn't like there were a lot of other options in El Paso. That was when I first became aware of the films of Stanley Kubrick. I saw his war movie *Fear and Desire* and then *Killer's Kiss.*

When I got out of the army and came back to New York and back to *Esquire* and ultimately to the job as art director at *Esquire,* everyone I knew was consumed by movies. Peter Bogdanovich was writing for *Esquire,* David Newman was an editor there, Dan Talbot was running the New Yorker Theater on upper Broadway, and, most important, Andrew Sarris was writing for *The Village*

Voice. We were seeing the first films of Bergman, Fellini, and Antonioni. The New Wave was just happening and there seemed to be a revolutionary new way to look at and think about films. The sense of ferment, the sense of excitement of those days, is impossible to describe. And it was just about then that I got fired from *Esquire*.

A friend of mine, Herb Sargent, had been offered $25,000 to write a treatment for a Doris Day movie. I thought if I could get my hands on that much money it would allow me to live until I figured out what I wanted to do with my life. There was only one catch: I didn't know how to write. In college I had taken one creative writing course and had flunked it. But I had a friend who was an editor at *Esquire* and a wonderful writer, David Newman. I went to David and spun out these dreams of the glamorous life of screenwriters. Next to telling my wife that I was an economically responsible human being when we got married, that was the greatest lie I ever told. Fortunately for me, David was as in love with movies as I was, so he took the bait.

By chance, at that time David and I happened to be reading a book by John Toland called *The Dillinger Days*. In the book there was a footnote about Bonnie Parker and Clyde Barrow. If I remember correctly, the footnote read, "Not only were they outlaws, but they were outcasts." That caught our attention.

Now my father, who was the world's most upright human being, had had two brothers, both of whom were involved in quasi-legal activities and both of whom had been murdered. My father had ducked that fate by moving to a larger city and marrying my mother and working for the telephone company all his life. He was the kind of man who would not cross the street if the light was red, but he was also a closet criminal. He read *True Detective* magazine regularly each month and, more important, went to the funerals of both Bonnie and Clyde; so I grew up, as did a lot of kids in Texas, with countless stories about Bonnie and Clyde. In the stories they were never regarded as vicious criminals, but as folk heroes. Those folk stories became the informing spirit of *Bonnie and Clyde*. John Ford was right in *The Man Who Shot Liberty Valance*— "Print the legend." Even so, David and I both knew that if we had been left alone in a room with Bonnie and Clyde, most likely they would have cheerfully killed us.

I think David and I felt that the line dividing a criminal and an upright citizen is much more subtle than most people realize, and certainly more subtle than most movies in those days led us to believe. We made a set of decisions, the first of which was to not pass moral judgment on our characters, and then to do our best to make the audience identify with them, and to see them as ordinary human beings just like us.

David and I didn't know how to write a screenplay. So we wrote a treatment that was eighty pages long—a very thorough treatment, filled with camera shots and indications of what people said. Although we didn't know how to write a screenplay, we *did* know who we wanted to direct it—François Truffaut. He had just done *400 Blows, Shoot the Piano Player*, and *Jules and Jim*. *Bonnie and Clyde*, at least in screenplay form, was deeply influenced by Truffaut. Well, we managed to get our treatment to a woman we knew named Helen Scott. She had been the head of the French Film Office in New York and had been instrumental in bringing Truffaut, Godard, Rohmer, and Charbol to this country at the height of the New Wave. She was a close friend of Truffaut, and by the time we sent her the treatment she was working for Lewis Allen preparing *Fahrenheit 451,* which Truffaut was scheduled to direct. She, in turn, sent our treatment on to Truffaut. In those days he didn't speak English, so he had the treatment translated into French and wrote us back saying that he was interested. He included a set of comic strips based on the story of Bonnie and Clyde that had been published, I believe, in *France Soir.* Well, two months later, he came to the United States on other business, and we sat in his hotel room for two or three days, with Helen acting as translator. We went through the treatment step by step, line by line. Whatever lessons we had in screenwriting all came from Truffaut. In the movie there's a sequence that he wrote line by line. It's when Bonnie reads her poem, "The Ballad of Bonnie and Clyde," and you see a series of dissolves from poem to the newspaper to Frank Hamer reading the newspaper to them in the field. Truffaut dictated that exactly. It was a wonderful time.

Anyway, there were two young people who optioned the treatment—Eleanor Jones and her brother Norton Wright—and they arranged for a screening of *Gun Crazy,* the Joseph Lewis noir film that Truffaut had suggested we see. We were sitting in the back of this theater with Truffaut and Helen, and in the front of the theater was Jean-Luc Godard. I thought I'd died and gone to heaven.

In any case we wrote the screenplay and sent it to Truffaut. He wrote back to say he liked it but that he'd already made the decision to direct *Fahrenheit* and couldn't make plans for more than one picture at a time. That was the bad news. The good news was that he also said he'd given it to his good friend Godard. We met with him, and he seemed anxious to do the film. Godard believed that American films were set up the way European films were, and that these two producers had the money to begin the picture right away. He said he wanted to make the movie, but that he needed to go back to France and get out of this picture that he really didn't want to do, *Alphaville*. He said he would and that he'd come back and could begin shooting the movie in December. Now, these producers were setting things up the way Americans do these things, by getting a script, then a director, and, with a director and a script, a star, and then with all that—the package—a deal with a studio. Naturally, Eleanor and Norton didn't want to admit to Godard that they didn't have the money to do it and that it was going to be a slower process than he expected. Instead, they said the film was written for the summer and that we should wait to make the film during the following summer. Well, Godard stood up and said, "I'm talking cinema, and you're talking meteorology." And he walked out the door. So for three to four years the picture sat. It was turned down by every major studio. The only studio, I think, that it never reached was Warner Bros.

Now it's about three years later. By then I'm married. The phone rings one morning and it's Warren Beatty, whom I'd gotten to know a little. He said he'd had lunch a week or so before with Truffaut, who told him there was a script he should read. In those days, the script included a ménage à trois between Bonnie, Clyde, and C. W., who was not the Michael J. Pollard character he became later; he was more of a dumb hunk. There were hints of bisexuality in it. So Warren came to our apartment, picked up the script, and called me back within twenty minutes to say, "I want to do it." I replied, "Warren, what page are you on?" He said, "Twenty-two." I said, "Wait till you get to page forty-four." About an hour and a half later he called and said, "I finished the script, I know what you mean, but I still want to do it." I told him who the producers were and he said that the option was due to lapse soon, and when it did he'd buy it. That's what happened.

Then Warren asked about our choice of a director and we said Godard or Truffaut. Wisely, he said, "You've already written a French screenplay. What you need is an American director." So we suggested Arthur Penn, who had done such remarkable films as *The Left Handed Gun* and *The Miracle Worker*. Warren and Arthur had just finished working on *Mickey One*. Warren thought about it and said, "I'm not so sure Arthur will want to work with me again, but I'm gonna lock myself in a room with him and I won't let him out until he agrees to do the picture." Sure enough, the next call we got was from Arthur. And the four of us—Warren, Arthur, David, and I—sat down and began to work on the script together. We learned a tremendous amount from Arthur. He is not only enormously talented, but he is also very articulate, and those two things don't go together very often. He taught us, among many other things, that not everything you write is actable. We learned how to construct characters and relationships that are playable. Because, when it comes down to it, as Robert Altman once said, "It all finally depends on the actors."

Somewhere along the way, Arthur came to us and said, "I want to take out the bisexuality." When our backs stiffened he said, "Here are the reasons. One, you've really written a heterosexual relationship. Two, whatever happens in this picture, the audience is bound to dismiss these people, saying, 'Oh, they're just a bunch of sexual deviants,' and I don't think that's what you want." He was right. Maybe in a novel that relationship might have worked; a novel is more interior and, as a reader, you can see what you want to see and not see what you don't want to see. But a movie doesn't work like that. Films are very literal. For instance, if I say to you that on the way to work this morning I saw the most beautiful woman I ever laid eyes on, you will instantly pull up your idea of the most beautiful woman you can imagine. If I show you a photograph of that woman, you will know exactly what I mean—but you may or may not think she is as beautiful as I do.

Warren and Arthur began shooting the picture in the fall and at a certain point Robert Towne was on the set and he made a huge and positive contribution to the film. I think if I had to pick five American screenplays from the latter half of the twentieth century from which to teach screenwriting, Robert's *Chinatown* would be near the top of the list.

When David and I saw a rough cut of *Bonnie and Clyde,* we both knew it was a movie to be enormously proud of, even though we kept hearing that the studio hated it. That the picture got released at all, and then re-released (which is when it became a real hit) is all due to Warren. I think it's impossible to overestimate his contribution to the film. Everyone forgets that when the picture opened it got devastating reviews. A week before *Bonnie and Clyde* opened I told my wife, "Look, you've got to know that even though we worked on it for a long time and even though we're very proud of it, it's just another movie. It will open, hang around a couple of weeks, and disappear like any other movie." After I read the reviews on opening day I wasn't sure it would make it for even a couple of weeks. Well, that's not totally true. Enough people had called us and said how much they loved it that we knew it was a good piece of work.

Somebody once asked me, "What is the common thread in the work you've done? What is it that links *Bonnie and Clyde, Kramer vs. Kramer, Places in the Heart,* and *Nobody's Fool?*" If I had to pick that common thread out of what I've done it would probably be the notion of family. Not the conventional idea of family of *Father Knows Best* or *Leave It to Beaver,* but a more complicated, more jerry-built arrangement that I find, nevertheless, very moving. The family in *Bonnie and Clyde* lives in a car. In *Bad Company* a bunch of kids heading west to avoid the Civil War make a kind of family. *The Late Show* begins with a man whose partner is killed and by the end he's formed another relationship, this one with a young woman. In *Kramer* Ted Kramer's wife leaves and he has to become father and mother to his child. In *Places* Edna Spalding's husband is killed at the beginning of the film and she has to make a new family for herself. Of course, somebody pointed this out to me after *Places* and made me more self-conscious and, therefore, less comfortable with that theme ever since.

When I started writing *Places in the Heart* it was with the intention of writing about my father's family, his two murdered brothers, and about the other people in the town. The script was to be based on the collection of different stories I'd heard as a child. I knew that one of the characters would be based on my great-grandmother, whose husband had been killed the Sunday before Christmas, leaving her four children to raise. And I knew there was going to be a character named Moze, though he wasn't forced to leave town. And I knew there was going to be a tornado. What happened was that the writing changed everything. Originally, I had the story of the woman whose husband was killed as a small story in this sort of gangster movie, but she forced her way into the foreground and pushed the gangsters out of the way. By the end of the third draft, there were no gangsters left.

What happens to me a lot is that the characters themselves take over; they acquire a heft, a size, a life of their own, and at some point they're often determined to do what they want to do regardless of what I have in mind. I listen to them—sometimes to my detriment, because sometimes the characters I write aren't smart enough to be in a movie.

In truth I'm not a very good storyteller; I'm a lot better

at character, because that's what fascinates me. It seems to me that there are two kinds of narratives; neither one is better than the other. There is the Hawksian film in which narrative is driven by character. That is to say, plot is determined by the character of the people in the story; *Rio Bravo* is probably the best example I know of that kind of story. Then there is the film in which character is determined by narrative. In a movie like *In Harm's Way* by Otto Preminger, character is a result of the things that happen to the people caught in the story. Much as I admire directors like Hitchcock and Preminger, I obviously find myself drawn to the films of Hawks and Renoir. Occasionally, of course, there are films that synthesize both of these threads; *Children of Paradise* is the best example I know of that.

Then the actor shows up. Once that happens the character is no longer someone who lives only inside my head. When I was reading *Nobody's Fool* by Richard Russo, I was not more than twenty pages into the book when I realized that for me, Sully was Paul Newman. So I wrote the film with Paul Newman's voice in my head. And as long as I'm on the subject of *Nobody's Fool,* I'd like to say a few things about Richard Russo. First of all, I think there is a huge difference between writing (as in writing novels) and screenwriting (as in writing screenplays). The easiest analogy is the difference between a painting and a blueprint. The painting, like the novel, is a thing in itself. But the blueprint or the screenplay points to something beyond itself. In the case of the blueprint it is an indispensable guide in the building of a house; in the case of the screenplay, it is a fundamental step in the making of a movie. Both the screenplay and the blueprint are a set of complex instructions on how to make a work of art (or commerce), but they are not the work of art itself; houses have been made without blueprints and movies have been made without screenplays. Consequently the demands made on a screenwriter are radically different than those made on a novelist, and sometimes those demands are antithetical. When I was doing the adaptation of *Nobody's Fool* I took a 500-page novel and reduced it to a 120-page screenplay. Needless to say I had to leave out a lot, and occasionally I invented other stuff to go in place of large chunks that were missing in order to move more directly from one point to another. When I turned in the screenplay to the producers (Scott Rudin and Arlene Donovan), they liked it and suggested changes. I made the changes, and then we began casting, preproduction, rehearsals, and finally shooting. One day, while we were shooting, Scott came to me and said, "Look, I hope you won't be offended, but I think in two or three of the scenes you've written you've lost the tone of Russo's novel; and one of the most beautiful parts of the novel is its tone." I said that I thought he was right, and Scott asked me if I'd object to asking Richard to take a crack at rewriting those scenes. I thought it was a great idea and called Richard right away. He agreed.

You know, I began my career as part of a writing team, but I had not worked with another writer for about twelve years, so I was very apprehensive. But what began then was a collaboration on what started out as three scenes,

then became four, and then five. And by the time we had
finished the picture there were more, I don't know how
many, but what I *do* know is that from my point of view
those are the best scenes in the picture. In fact, the work
was good enough, and I had had such a good time, that
I asked Richard if he would consider collaborating again,
this time on an original. That became *Twilight,* and now
we're considering another collaboration. This is a long
and complicated way of saying that Richard is one of the
only people I know who understands the demands and the
possibilities of both screenplays and novels.

On my own I don't think I'm a particularly good writer,
but I'm determined and I'm persistent. I write and I rewrite and I rewrite and I rewrite. Very early on I read
something that Neil Simon had written in the *Dramatist's
Guild Quarterly.* I don't remember the quote exactly, but
in essence he said that when he was writing *The Odd
Couple* he rewrote the poker scene thirty or thirty-five
times. He said the important thing to keep in mind was
not how many unsuccessful drafts he had already written,
but what he wanted the scene to be. That changed my
whole point of view about screenwriting. Until then, I
thought of writing in terms of a studio contract: first draft,
polish, second draft, polish, and that's it. But, in my case
at least, that's not a very realistic way of writing. In my
case the first draft merely blocks in the characters, roughs
in a story line that works, and hopefully establishes a beginning and an ending that is satisfactory. In other words,
it tells me that, possibly, with a great deal of work, there
is a movie in there somewhere. The really interesting work

starts with the second draft and the rewrites that come after that. Then I have the freedom to try out all sorts of ideas and discard the ones that make me cringe. I also depend a lot on the input of my producers and a handful of people I trust.

I remember when we were doing *Places*. The script had been done and we were well into casting when I spoke with Carol Littleton, the editor. At that time the script had Edna Spalding's sister and another woman in the town who was a beautician whose husband was having an affair. Carol said that these two women overlapped one another and that it might be much more effective to combine them into one character. The minute she said that I wondered why I hadn't seen that before, and I immediately made the change. Another example, in *Kramer,* was also in preproduction. In the script, at that point there was not only the character of Margaret, the neighbor who lived downstairs, but also her husband (Charley) from whom she was separated. Arlene Donovan, who along with Sam Cohn represented me (she later became my producer, from *Still of the Night* through *Twilight*), pointed out that ultimately the character of Charley was going to get cut from the film because, no matter how much I liked him, he was outside the narrative line of the film. When she said it, I didn't want to hear it, but she was right and when I actually cut him out there was a great feeling of relief. It is very exciting when you feel the picture get better, and I suppose that's what allows me to keep my enthusiasm through rewrite after rewrite.

Now, the opposite of this is a quote I once heard, I

think it was attributed to Harriet Frank and Irving Rav-etch: "We like to think we got it right the first time."

My later drafts are usually done after the picture is cast (often during the shooting) because I think it is critically important that the writer take into account the actors' voices. As Dustin Hoffman said, "There is acting and there is behavior, and it is almost impossible to act behavior." For instance you can tell as many jokes as you want, but you cannot act wit. Paul Newman has it, so do John Malkovich, Bruce Willis, and Susan Sarandon. But there are many other fine actors who don't have a clue. In rehearsal and during the shooting you get to know the actors and get to their behavior and it is always my impulse to try to incorporate that behavior into the character whenever possible. As an example, when we were preparing *Kramer* I knew that Dustin liked to work with a certain amount of freedom; he didn't like to feel as though he were in a straitjacket. So Stanley Jaffe, the producer, and Dustin and I met for a week in Stanley's hotel suite, working our way through the script line by line—and I taped it all. By the time we were finally finished I had caught the rhythm of Dustin's speech and rewrote the script with Dustin's speech patterns in mind. This allowed Dustin the freedom he needed during shooting and made me look like less of a schmuck as a director.

The fact is that I try to solve a lot of the directing problems during the writing, and I try my best to give the actors freedom. Because I sincerely believe that there is a very good chance that they will find things—wonderful things—in the characters I wrote, and that these will be things I never dreamed of, and that the picture will be richer for it. I've come to believe that ninety percent of directing is casting, and that you hire actors not simply because they give good line readings, but for their intelligence. We must trust that intelligence.

Finally, I get asked all the time about the last scene in *Places in the Heart,* the one in which all the people who have died show up during the church service that ends the film. Here's how it happened: When I grew up in this little town in Texas my mother was religious, but I wasn't. However, somewhere along the way, when I was in my mid-forties I began to go to church again regularly. Well, one Sunday when I was in the midst of the earliest draft of the movie, when Edna Spalding was barely in the picture, I was sitting in church and they passed around one of those trays filled with little glasses of grape juice. Suddenly, out of nowhere, that last scene of the film just showed up. Suddenly I saw a scene in a movie (that I hadn't yet written) that took place in a church in a small town in Texas, in the middle of the Depression, where for a moment the living and the dead mingled together. And what that signified for me was some kind of profound hope. That scene was a gift. I didn't earn it, I didn't figure it out or think it through; it just showed up. Like most of the best parts of my life, it was a gift.

RON BASS

I met Ron at his gorgeous home and was struck by how completely unpretentious he seemed. He is, after all, probably the most prolific screenwriter working today. Knowing that he had once been a lawyer, I began the interview by asking the obvious: What made you leave the law and begin writing?

I WAS SICK AS A KID, BEDRIDDEN FOR MANY YEARS WITH an array of very strange symptoms—bizarre stuff that nobody could figure out and that I just seemed to outgrow by the time I was ten or eleven. What I was left with was a permanently enhanced imagination and a great love of reading. My heroes were Dostoyevsky, Faulkner, and Fitzgerald, and what I wanted most to be in life was a novelist. In fact, I wrote a novel when I was in high school and didn't show it to anybody until I took freshman English from a wonderful teacher. She read it and was very encouraging about my talent, but she didn't ever lead me to believe that the novel itself was good enough to be published.

Well, being young and passionate, I burned the only copy of the novel and went on with my life. If all you want is to play center field for the Yankees and you know when you're seventeen that you're obviously not good enough to do that—that you're really just an ordinary person and not extraordinary like Joe DiMaggio or Mickey Mantle—you find other things to do. Me, I wanted to write another *Great Gatsby*. And I wasn't good enough. So I looked elsewhere.

I majored in philosophy and got a masters in international relations, because I wanted to be in the foreign service and travel. Then I decided to go to law school as a way of keeping my options open. At the end of my second year (at Harvard Law School), law firms came recruiting. Some of them were from my hometown, Los Angeles, and that's how I learned that there was this thing called entertainment law. Going into entertainment law, I decided, would bring me into close proximity to writers and artists, and also I'd get to be around movies, which I loved. So that's what I did.

It was the late 1960s—an interesting time in entertainment. I specialized in negotiating deals; I was a dealmaker. I loved it and was good at it, but I knew instinctively that something was missing, so sometime in the early seventies I started writing a new version of the novel that I'd torched. Eventually, I got it published, and that was wonderful, even though it didn't sell all that many copies. So I kept writing in my spare time while still practicing law. Every two years I'd write another novel. I'd write on weekends, on vacations, on planes; I just loved doing it.

Then we had some financial problems, my wife and I, mostly from a very bad investment that kept bleeding us. So when I heard about an opportunity to write a World War II novel based on a news clip the *Reader's Digest* condensed-book lady gave me, and to possibly sell the book for a lot of money, I woke up at three every morning, for two months, to write an extensive treatment; I figured this book was my best chance to get out of the hole.

Really, the most I was hoping for was an advance of $25,000, which would've bailed me out. I gave the treatment to my agent—and then decided that I should do what I do best. I said, "I'll tell you how to negotiate this." I did—and we ended up with $60,000.

When the book was completed, a friend of mine named Melinda Jason took a copy of the galleys to Jonathan Sanger, who'd produced *The Elephant Man*. He hadn't directed a film yet but wanted to, and thought he could use this material. Not having a film agent, I negotiated my own deal to be hired to write the screenplay from my novel. I'd never thought about writing a screenplay before. It's not that I thought it was below me; I'd thought only about writing fiction. But now here was this chance to write a screenplay for a lot of money. And that was the incentive.

The name of the book was *The Emerald Illusion*. It was a spy novel, about an Allied overlord who's captured by the Germans and has to be rescued before he divulges what he knows about D Day. I modeled it after John Le Carré, so it was a novel about characters who just happened to be spies. But the people who eventually financed the film liked World War II movies and they were turning it into a World War II action-suspense movie. I didn't know that at the time. I only knew that the thing was being shot and I hadn't heard from them for a long time. So, with great moxie, I told them I wanted to be on the set. That was something I'd actually negotiated into my contract. Now, the fact that they were shooting in Paris was a great incentive to want to be there. But I also wanted to see what they were doing with my script.

This was 1984, and my second child had just been born, and now here I am, in my favorite city, thinking about how incredibly fortunate I am—and then I notice people treating me kind of funny. Finally I asked to see the shooting script, and that's when they told me that it had been rewritten by *several* people. I hadn't known about any of them. When I saw the script, I was very disheartened. I thought they'd taken the heart out of it. True, there was probably a lot more in there of mine than I gave them credit for, but at the time I was devastated. Still, this was Paris, and I decided to stay for the rest of the shoot, which was three more weeks. So here I am, hanging out with Ed Harris and Max von Sydow and Eric Stoltz, eating great French lunches. And then one morning Max comes up to me and begins talking about some of the dialogue his character is supposed to be saying in his scenes that day, and I sort of rewrite it for him, to his taste. Well, he takes the rewrites to Jonathan, who actually used some of it, and that was a great feeling. It got to be a regular thing, and after a few days, Ed Harris came up and said, "I hear you and Max talk all the time. Do you think maybe you and I could . . ." That's how I wound up being a guerilla in my own movie.

Anyway, what I learned is that writing screenplays is every bit as much fun as writing novels, plus you're getting paid a lot more money. I also liked the discipline of having to compress a story into as few pages as possible. You have to get rid of much of the material that you ordinarily put in a novel—and that can work in a novel but not a screenplay. A screenplay is about distilling the essence of a story and its characters. You really have to find the heart and soul of your story and hew to it. The difference between books and movies is that books are about what happens within people, and movies are about what happens *between* people.

The experience on *Code Name: Emerald,* which is what they called the movie, pretty much hooked me on being a screenwriter. Pretty soon I'd made a deal at Fox. They pitched me ideas, and I turned them into screenplays, but because I was still a lawyer, I had to do them all in whatever free time I could manage.

I was so ambitious and so determined, I didn't mind getting up at three in the morning, writing from three to six, then playing with my kids, going to the office at eight, working until six, and then going back to writing after dinner and on weekends. In that way I wrote four scripts in a year and a half, while still practicing law.

It wasn't a burden or onerous, because I love to write. I really do love it. When I go out into the garden with some pencils and a pad of paper and my imagination, nothing else exists. Even when I'm not actually writing,

I'm still working. I'm always working on my stories. I think about them *all* the time. I think about them when I'm sleeping and when I wake up in the morning. The minute my eyes open, I'll just lie there and think about the first scene I'm going to write that day, and I'll finally get up when I just have to go and write everything down.

Eventually I got to the point where I was devoting less time to law than I used to, and my billable hours were down. It became clear that I was soon going to have to choose between being a full-time writer and a full-time lawyer. That was when Joe Wizan at Fox came to me and said, "How many deals do you have waiting for you?" I said four. And he said, "How many more would you need to have for you to quit the practice of law and write full-time?" I said, "Well, if I had two more blind deals of X amount of dollars, I guess I wouldn't be able to resist quitting." So that's what happened.

I knew that that first year was going to be a good year financially. But there were no guarantees after that. This was in June of 1984. And, thank God, I haven't looked back or regretted my decision for a day. I still always look forward to writing; I'm always engaged by it and thrilled to be in the process. I could sit on a plane to Hong Kong or Paris for twelve hours, and work every single minute and not be aware of the time. I use pencil and loose-leaf notebook paper, and usually sit outside, away from phones or anything else to distract me and bring me back to earth.

But the truth is that screenwriting is not just art or pleasure, it's also business. I finally figured that out in 1993, when we were making *The Joy Luck Club*. Until then I'd considered myself a "writer's writer," like a novelist. And with that attitude I found it difficult to handle the studios. I really resisted changing my scripts with their notes, and thought of the struggle between us as a competition: Who was going to prevail? No wonder I was always divorced from the filmmaking process, because once they took the script away from me and delivered it to the set, I didn't feel welcome and no longer cared to be part of the process anyway. This thing they were shooting wasn't my "novel" anymore. And then I became a producer on *The Joy Luck Club*—and had a kind of epiphany that enabled me to see how wrong my attitude had been.

It was because of my childhood dream of being a novelist that I wanted to think of myself as a writer, but screenwriting isn't simply writing. When you're a screenwriter, you're a filmmaker. That doesn't mean it's better or worse than being a writer's writer, but it is different. You're part of a team, a team that includes the actors and producers and director and cinematographer and editor and even studio executives. Everyone contributes to the process, and if you're going to survive as a screenwriter with your sanity intact, you have to divorce yourself from the idea that you're in charge of your script and give yourself over to the idea that the director is the boss. The moment you do, you can look at the notes you're given in a different way, and can work with them constructively.

Before, I looked at notes and other people's ideas as intrusions; that was the filter for me, the idea that they were taking away my baby and turning it into a monster.

Yes, if someone presented something to me that on first blush I could see was better than what I had, I was always thrilled and would accept it gratefully. But if I didn't see the improvement right away, I resisted the change. Only when I became a producer did I understand that the director is the person who has to work with the material, and if he or she isn't comfortable with it and doesn't share its vision, the film is going to suffer. So what this epiphany did was turn me into a collaborator. I realized that I'm not writing a script that's intended to sit on a shelf and be read by a lucky few. What I'm writing is the action and the words that will be depicted in a film that will, one hopes, be seen by millions; the words on the page are not the film. As a screenwriter, I can't divorce myself from the film itself; I have to understand everyone else's needs— from the executives to the financial backers. Any screenwriter who thinks that he should be given a blank check to write art would do better to write plays or books, the two mediums where his word is law.

What's funny is when people I haven't worked with in a few years have notes for me, especially on a first draft. And because I'm sort of visible now and have an Oscar, they dread having to tell *Ron Bass* that they think they can make his script better. So they're always amazed and delighted when I say, "Okay, great, let's hear it!" The only thing I tell them is, "Don't give me a memo; don't write out the notes. I'll sit with you for twenty-seven hours and hear everything you want to say, but I do not want to read about it on paper." If we are really partners and collaborators, I want to behave that way. I'm not interested in saying no unless no is really the right answer. I'm looking to make everyone, including myself, happy. I try to make the director my friend. The closer we are, the more involved I'm going to be in the filming process—and the more of my work I'll recognize when it hits the screen.

Yes, I enjoy all the writing, but I enjoy adaptations most. The reason is that there are already a wonderful story and characterizations to use as a sort of treatment. What's great for the film you get to keep, and what's not you throw away. More than that, though, the executives and producers you're dealing with already have a decent expectation of what the finished story is going to look like, because they've already bought the book.

Naturally, you give them your take on the source material. You say, "This is what I'm doing differently. This is what doesn't work in the book for the movie's sake. Here are brand new things that I'm inventing. Here's how I'm gonna structure it. Here's what's got to be different." So they know what you're thinking, and that's why you get the job, because either their thinking is the same as yours, or they like your thinking. It's the same when you go in to rewrite someone else's script. You need to have a good mind meld with the producer or studio. You say, "I like this, and this I don't like, this has got to change, this has got to move over here, this I'm gonna do a little bit differently, this I'm gonna preserve and I'm gonna do it this way." And they understand what you're saying, because there's source material to use as a common point of reference.

Now, when I do an original, it's like a chunk of clay.

Nothing is formed and everything has to be shaped. Which means of course that there's always going to be an enormous rewrite from first to second draft. It doesn't matter if when I pitched the story I pitched every single scene exactly the way I wrote it, because it always looks different from what they thought they were buying before I went off to write it. But when that first draft is finally in everyone's hands, we can all work on it together, so that their ideas and my ideas mesh. I understand that that's the game. Because no one on the studio end has the ability to give you notes *before* they see a first draft. Once we have that first draft, we can all get down and work together. Then they start to feel better. We refine and refine and refine.

My Best Friend's Wedding was an original—a complete, spec original. The idea behind it was actually a few different ideas that just happened to coalesce over a period of time. The first part of the chain was the wedding of a friend's son I'd gone to years ago in Chicago. It was a Jewish wedding, one of those four-day affairs, with people from all over the country. I was just fascinated by watching all the politics and stuff going on. Then, sometime later, an agent of mine showed me a magazine article about a woman who heard that her ex-boyfriend had gotten married and she was wistfully remembering her romance with him years before and sort of regretting that maybe she hadn't taken a chance at marrying him when she could have. And I said to the agent, "Well, that's not a movie, it's not a story, there's no story there. Somebody sitting back and remembering something is not a story. A story would be if she'd heard about it *before* the guy got married and decided she wanted to go do something about it—maybe even go to the wedding and disrupt it."

Anyway, that was that; these were just two ideas floating in the mental soup of ideas. And they remained there until I mentioned them to my team—the people I employ as a sort of private development group. They help me refine my ideas and scripts. What happened was, I said to one of them that I wanted to do a story about a hero or heroine who *doesn't* get the girl or guy. I said that because I'm always looking for a way to reverse conventional storytelling expectations. I said, "I want to work it out so that you take the audience on a ride and suddenly the audience starts to not even want the heroine to get the guy. Because the other gal is so terrific and she's not a bitch, so it's not like *Sleepless in Seattle,* where you see that Meg Ryan's fiancé, Bill Pullman, is kind of a nothing, so of course she's gonna wind up with Tom Hanks. But what if Bill Pullman had been every bit as cool as Tom Hanks? What if he had been even cooler and you really weren't sure that what was right for Meg Ryan was to be with Tom Hanks, but you love Tom Hanks and you didn't want him to not get the girl? What if they don't get together after all?"

From out of that, articulating what I wanted to see, the two bigger ideas came together. It became: "She goes back to get the guy away from his bride and doesn't get him back. Yes, she tries to, she wants to, but she fails, and it's right that she fails and the audience feels good that she fails even though they feel bad for her and she runs and blah, blah, blah." The final piece of the puzzle was figuring out that the friend who helps her was gay. At the time there were not a lot of movies with straight girls and gay guys. Now, I guess, it's become a cliché.

The funny thing about *My Best Friend's Wedding* is that it didn't have to be a comedy. It could've been dramatic and heartrending. But I wanted it to be a kind of Lucy Ricardo, goofy thing, with her trying to break things up, and everything she does backfiring, and then even when it doesn't backfire, it backfires.

In the end, I think, it was touching, too. I like to write stuff like that—stuff like *Rain Man,* which is comedic and dramatic and poignant and full of conflict. You want to give the audience the full, dynamic range of emotions.

Rain Man began as an idea of Barry Morrow's. He'd written I don't know how many drafts of a script that was similar in a lot of ways to what it became, but different in a lot of ways, too. For one thing, the Rain Man character was not autistic; he was retarded, an idiot savant. So his personality was the opposite of the movie character. He was lovable and sweet and puppy-dog-like and always wanted to hold your hand. The brother, instead of being much younger like Tom Cruise, was around the same age, maybe two years younger than Raymond. And he was just irritated that this guy was always hanging on to him and always kissing up to him, like an innocent little puppy dog.

Well, the studio didn't like the script but loved the idea, and Roger Birnbaum asked me if I could put other things I was doing aside in order to undertake this project. I loved the idea, and of course Dustin Hoffman and Tom were already attached. The funny thing was, I'd just caught the chicken pox from my older daughter. It was a bad, bad case—no fun at all. Marty Brest, who was the director then, had a pregnant wife, and Dustin's wife was pregnant, too, so I couldn't be in the same room with Dustin or Marty for fear of giving them the virus, which they'd then pass on. So everything was done by phone between me and Marty; he was giving me all the notes. Then he put Dustin and Tom on the phone with me, and Dustin said, "Did it ever cross your mind that, instead of being retarded, he might be autistic? Did you ever think of that? Is that something that would even appeal?" Marty just kind of cut him off, in a very nice way but cut him off all the same, and when the actors were off the phone I said to Marty that when an actor says something like that to the writer, he's probably thought a lot about it and he means it. Marty said he'd take care of it, because he didn't want too many voices in the mix. He said, "You're working with me, you're doing a great job, I'll deal with Dusty and everything's going to be fine," and so on. So I finished my draft, then went off to Hawaii to meet my family for spring break. When I came back I learned that Marty Brest had left the project because of creative differences. I thought, how sad, because I *loved* the project.

That summer I was staying in Paris with my family and I got a call from Mike Ovitz. We thought the project was dead, dead, dead, deader than a doornail, but he said that Steven Spielberg wanted to direct the movie and wanted to bring me on. He said, "Can you come back and meet with Steven Spielberg?" Amazingly, I said, "No, I'm with my family in Paris," and told him I was coming back on such and such a day, and if he could wait till then, great; if not, well, I'd promised my family and that came first. Pretty ballsy, huh? But it turned out to be fine, and when I came back I did meet with Steven. The first thing he said to me after hello was, "Dustin Hoffman is right and you're wrong. Do you want to know why?" I said sure. He said, "Isn't this story just a love story between two brothers?" I said absolutely. He said, "What's the most important thing in a love story? It's the obstacle that keeps the loves apart and that has to be overcome." I said that I totally agreed. He said, "Well, if the guy's retarded and lovable and always holding your hand, yeah, sure, it's annoying, but you know that, eventually, with this character the audience loves so much already, the brother will love him, too, so there's no real obstacle. The way it is now, the brother's just being a hard-ass and eventually the guy will break through. However, if he's autistic and he's a jerk and it's really difficult to like him, and he won't look you in the eye and he won't let you touch him and he's really a pain in the ass—*now* you've got a real obstacle." And I said the only thing I could say. I said, "You're totally right. In fact, maybe you're even too right. Maybe it's too big an obstacle." And he said, "No, no, no. It's all in the casting. Dustin Hoffman will make you love him, even when he's being completely true to character as an autistic. He can be the most annoying guy in the world, but you're still gonna love him. There's no way you won't love that guy." And that's the way it turned out.

Eventually, Steven left the picture. What happened was, Steven and Dustin and Tom and I worked on the script all during the summer of 1987, in a beach house in Malibu. All of them were wonderful—joys to work with. And then one day Steven came in and said he had to pull out because he'd promised George Lucas he'd start the next *Raiders* sequel on the first of April. He said, "Where we are on this script and the work that we still have to go, I'm never gonna get it and do the film and get everything done in time to do that."

Obviously, I thought the project was dead, over, jump off the cliff. Then Ovitz calls and says Sydney Pollack now wants to do the film. I said, "Well, then, I'm toast," because I know he likes to work with Kurt Luedtke and David Rayfiel. He said, "Well, yeah, he's gonna fire you. But he wants to know if you'll come down to Universal and meet with him for a day so he can pick your brain." I know that sounds brutal and cruel, but I got it totally and appreciated it. By this point I was invested emotionally, and I wanted to see the movie done, even if I wasn't the one writing it. Nobody held a gun to my head. And in fact, I found my day with Sydney Pollack to be wonderful. He was honest, straightforward, and really smart. And what I learned was that he was making the right decision to fire me, because I couldn't have done what he wanted done.

What happened next is that his guys couldn't make the script work, and there was a Writers Guild strike looming; it's the winter of 1988. And now I get another call from Ovitz saying that Barry Levinson wants to direct this movie—and wants me to come back on the project. Working with him was totally different from working with Steven, but equally wonderful. Like Steven, Barry is, of course, a writer. Anyway, the strike date is getting closer and closer, and I actually hand-delivered my last handwritten pages to his front door at seven in the morning on the morning the strike was supposed to begin at ten. I didn't ring the bell and wake him up. I just took a rock and put the last yellow pages under the rock, left, and never talked to him again—I was on strike! I didn't go to the set to see what was being shot.

The ending of the film, the last shot, has a story that I think is pretty instructive about the business and the way different people see the same material through different perspectives. The ending that Barry shot has Tom walking away from the train that is taking Dustin back to the home, and then the screen fades to black. That was the ending I wrote for Barry, the one he wanted. The one I wrote for Steven Spielberg, the one he wanted, had Tom's girlfriend, Valeria Golino, back in his life at that point and going with him to see Raymond off at the train, for his trip home. And Dustin was going to come apart emotionally because Tom's not going back East with him, and Tom was going to say to him as they're standing on the steps of the train, "Don't be nervous, don't worry, I'm coming in two weeks and I'm going to see you in two weeks at the home, we're going to have a great time, we're going to play ball and I'm going to keep coming and I'm going to come a lot and I'm going to see you a lot." But it wasn't appeasing Dustin because his character doesn't get the concept of the future; he only knows that his brother's not going now. And so the train starts up and Dustin's really losing it, and as the train starts to pull out Tom looks to his girlfriend and the girlfriend just nods, and Tom grabs the train, puts one foot on the thing, and the train pulls out with Tom sort of hanging half off it.

I really liked that ending, and if Steven had directed the movie, that's how it would have been. But Barry felt it was too happy, too up, because the bottom line was that these two brothers were never going to live together. Raymond, Dustin's character, was always going to have to be institutionalized; he couldn't be adopted and live with Tom. Tom was going to have to live his life and come visit now and then. So Barry didn't want the ending to change the viewer's perception of the future between the brothers. The question was, Do you want to leave on the up, or do you want to leave with the reality that Tom can't be in Dustin's life?

For Barry Levinson, *Rain Man* is the story of two men who could never really have a relationship. Raymond wasn't capable of a real relationship. And therefore it was always a story about Tom, and of seeing his face, the way he'd changed. There was nowhere else to go; it had to end on the character who'd gone through the change, whose story it really was.

For me, though, it was the story of a relationship, which is why I wanted to end on the *relationship,* which I saw as the level of connection that had been achieved between the brothers. Now, some screenwriters would probably feel cheated, thinking that the most important scene in the movie, the one that people take away from the theaters with them, was butchered or something like that. I don't. Not in the least. Because I realize that that's the decision you make when you become a screenwriter. You give up the power to determine the final choice. The joys and benefits of being part of a collaborative effort, and of getting the input and the genius of a Barry Levinson and a Steven Spielberg and a Dustin Hoffman and a Tom Cruise and other people, allow you to do better work than you'd probably do on your own; you have the satisfaction of contributing something important to something important. It's a joint effort, like a good marriage. You can't have a good marriage if you've got to win all the time or if you're unhappy every time something goes down that wasn't the way you'd prefer it. If you're keeping score, don't be married.

Now we fast-forward to the night of the Oscars, when I won. I took my statue and went backstage, and the first person I saw in the wings was Tom Cruise, whom I really didn't know other than working with him that summer. And here's Tom, who didn't win an Oscar and really deserved to win one, and he looks at me with that trademark Tom Cruise grin, the grin that women die for the world over, and he comes over with his arms out and lifts me up and swings me around. I was flabbergasted, because here's a guy who has every right to feel that everybody else in this thing is being rewarded for a job well done, and his part of the job was so essential, and not only was his performance essential, but he'd hung in there and turned down twenty-seven other films over all these years to stick with Dusty, so his pal and hero Dustin Hoffman could have this movie that Dustin wanted so desperately—and he's happy for me! Amazing. I will always remember that moment. What a mensch he is.

You know, I sometimes have to remind myself that I was that sick little kid, stuck in bed, reading book after book and traveling to far-off worlds only in my mind. In some sense, that experience informs everything I write, but not in the ordinary way, I don't think, that traumatic or difficult times shape an artist, especially writers. For me it has much more to do with learning to live with myself in my imagination. I made my imagination a place where I'm comfortable. I can live with my own feelings and my own depth of feelings and my ability to role-play—to be all these different people and be them in a natural, unself-conscious way. When I write it's really like auto-writing; it's not quite a conscious act where I have to think, "And then he says and she says." No, I'm not doing that; I just *am* everybody. I'm being it and watching it and am not even aware that there's a process going on. I'm told by people who've seen me when I write that my mouth moves. I guess I'm doing the dialogue. I'm not aware of it, but I'm obviously saying it.

What I don't have to think about is scene structure, because by the time I start writing, that's all taken care of. It's all planned in the preparation. For me, the most important part of the writing process is the outlining and the blocking out and the coming up with ideas and handling all the smaller things that are put in the notes before beginning that thing we call writing.

I used to do the scene-by-scene outlines alone. Now I do them with my creative team. They offer me a lot of things. They play devil's advocate to my ideas, give me some of their own, tell me when I've gone astray from the original concept, and provide companionship. It's a very lonely thing, writing is. And feedback is healthy. The way it works is, I usually come to them with an outline that I'm pitching, and I pitch it to them. They may comment, but usually not too much at this point, because the idea is still fluid. Then we go through blocking, dissecting every scene and talking about what I want in it. Then they start to make suggestions. Then I get memos from them as to everything that's been said. And then the four of them, the core crew of four, send me a fax of their ideas pertaining to every single component. You see, each of them has a different personality and comes to the material with a different prism. They may just send jokes or dialogue snatches or ideas or set-dressing, or they may criticize the way I laid things out—you know, "Instead of the thing happening by the tree, I think it should be by the river." Or, "I think she should be angry instead of happy." They'll also do research, finding out what it looks like where the scene's supposed to be set, or different things about birds, if it's a bird-watching moment.

The truth is, I often don't read everything they send me. There'll be scenes where I'll actually read all the blocking, mine and theirs, before I ever write a word. But at the other end of the spectrum, there are times when I read nothing, including my own notes. I just write the scene and never look back and never read it or anything else in between. Sometimes I just read my own stuff before I write, and sometimes I'll read my own stuff and one or two of theirs. Sometimes I write it without reading anything but then I go back and read the scene again before I let go of it to see if there is something that somebody has said that I want to change and include. It's an art, not a science; it's done by feel and instinct. You know when you want stimulation and when you don't want it, but I like not having to begin with a completely empty page. In fact, I worked this way before I ever had my own team; I had my own notes, accumulated over time, so I never had to really face the "Oh, my God, what do I do here?" blank page. Ideas beget ideas, which is why some of the most interesting ideas come out of conversations with people you don't necessarily agree with. Looking at ideas on a page stimulates your own thinking. In the end, though, when I write I'm writing alone.

I still get up at three-thirty or four every morning and try to stop at dinner and not work after dinner. And I work outside, if possible, in my yard or in Jane's yard— she's one of the senior members of my team. I do that because I can bring in scenes when I'm done with them and show them to her. Then I send the scenes to someone else who types them up and sends them to everyone else, so that I can get immediate feedback. I want it right away, because two days later I don't want somebody's comment about hating it; by then, I'm too far downstream.

As far as I know, no other screenwriter uses or has used this kind of team concept. But in a way it's essentially what happens in the development process at a studio. My way, the process is speeded up by a thousand percent, plus I'm in control of the development. You know, the development process at the studios is really backward. They should just let writers write and get that first draft in, not try to micromanage the writing before it's even written.

I actually don't know why more writers don't do it this way. True, not all that many can afford to do what I'm doing, but everybody, every writer, aspiring or accomplished, knows at least one or two people who can offer legitimate criticisms and feedback—which is what every writer needs. Whether it's your wife or your husband or your uncle, you have to have unfawning, unadorned criticism. Even Hemingway had Max Perkins. Of course, if you have a Max Perkins in your life, you don't need anybody else.

MICHAEL BLAKE

Michael and I spoke by phone from his home in Arizona. He had just sold the movie rights to his novel *The Holy Road,* a sequel to *Dances with Wolves,* for an impressive amount of money to a German company, which plans to mount an elaborate production. My first question was about the last scene in *Dances with Wolves,* in which the character of Dances with Wolves leaves the Indian camp with his wife, Stands with a Fist, in order to keep the army from slaughtering all the Indians in camp. It had always seemed to me that the army would pursue a scorched-earth policy anyway, whether or not Dances with Wolves was there.

YOU KNOW, THAT WAS PROBABLY THE BIGGEST BATTLE I had with Kevin and Jim Wilson (the film's producer). I think for that particular movie the ending worked very well; the public really liked it; but I still think it was rather muddled—it wasn't made clear—that he was supposed to be going off to find help or something. In the book, Dances with Wolves goes up to Ten Bears and announces his intention to leave, and Ten Bears says, "I'll think it over," and when he comes back he walks into Dances with Wolves's lodge and says, "I don't really see a white man here; I just see a Comanche warrior." So there is no Lieutenant Dunbar anymore, and that's the way it was left. But I do think the movie's ending was effective, at least in terms of the impact that it had on the audience.

Sometimes movies don't have to make complete sense. If you have a really solid movie, a movie that keeps the audience engaged throughout, they're much more likely to skip over anything that might be questionable or a cop-out or weak at the end. Obviously, it would be better not to do that, but sometimes a movie is about emotion, not logic, and it's the emotion that carries the moment.

I came to Hollywood at the end of 1979 to pursue a career as a screenwriter, and was able to get only one small story on the screen as a low-budget movie, in 1982. It had various titles—originally *Double Down,* which the distributor changed to *Stacy's Knights.* Kevin Costner starred in it and Jim Wilson directed it. After that I spent the next ten years really committed to writing screenplays, and while my writing was perceived as very good, it was considered by the film community to be too literate. The reaction I got from most people was that the screenplays read like books. I hadn't written any books then, but the thought was probably planted in my mind by all the comments. Only in Hollywood is "literate" not a compliment.

My first novel was *Dances with Wolves,* in 1986, which I basically wrote at the behest of Kevin Costner. It came from a kind of half-baked idea for a film that had been inspired by reading a lot of American Indian history, particularly from the period of the 1850s on up to the reservation period. What sprouted was this little seed of an idea that I took over to Kevin's house one evening. We had spaghetti, he and his wife and I, and we were just shooting the breeze, and I mentioned this germ of an idea I had, which I thought would make a great movie. Kevin was getting to be pretty much in demand at the time, so he had a stack of scripts at the side of the living room— and there beside the stack was a paperback novel. He said, "See that? Don't write a screenplay, because it'll just go in that stack. Better to write a book; it'll stand alone." He was very adamant about it, and even grabbed me by the shirt as I left, saying, "Write a book. Write a book." So a couple of weeks later I started to write a book—and of course everybody said, "Well, it reads like a movie."

My basic problem as a writer in the earlier years, and it continues somewhat today, is that as a novelist I'm considered by the Eastern publishing establishment to be more of a movie writer, and as a movie writer I'm considered by the Hollywood establishment to be more of a novelist. I pretty much ignore that, because I consider myself to be a storyteller—and I don't think it matters what form the stories take.

To tell you the truth, I really, really enjoy writing novels, but the pull of the movies is also still very strong for me because the medium has tremendous power. And from an American point of view, it really hasn't been fully tapped. Also, most of the movies that become classics are produced not because of the system but in spite of the system. I still have hope for the movies and that's why I'm still in that arena. However, I would say that I probably get more satisfaction from writing a novel, simply because there's less handling of a novel; novelists are considered to be a little more like playwrights, in that their work isn't as tampered with. When you write a film, you're opening yourself up, because everyone from the most humble mailroom trainee to the biggest producer feels that they have a kind of inside track on what a movie should be. There's an old joke about this that I don't think is a joke: The producer has a meeting of his staff, holds up a screenplay in the air, and tells everyone what a great screenplay it is. Then he says, "Now, who can we get to rewrite it?" That is the inherent difficulty of the writer in Hollywood; the writing is always considered to be basically a blueprint that is then tailored to fit the needs of stars, producers, directors, studio executives, and on and on.

I'll tell you how I got started in Hollywood. I'd gone to film school with Jim Wilson, and we'd both relocated to L.A. One night I ran into him at a birthday party and he asked me what it would take to write a screenplay. At the time I was living in a loft downtown and had no money, so I came up with the astronomical amount of $400 a week for something like eight weeks. He agreed to pay it, and I wrote the script for *Double Down*. We worked on it together somewhat, with Jim giving me ideas. His original idea was a courtroom drama with a couple of women on trial for trying to break the bank at a casino. My idea was that the courtroom drama would be rather staid and lifeless; it was taking on a subject, a legal subject, that I didn't think would have much appeal, so what I came up with was a story about a mousy young girl who overcomes her shyness because she has a gift.

When the script was finished, Jim went out on his own and raised about a quarter of a million dollars. That was when we met Kevin. He came to an open casting call and was head and shoulders above everyone else we were seeing, so Jim cast him as the lead in that movie. We went up to Reno, Nevada, and shot it, brought it back, and figured we had made it. But every distributor rejected it, and then for some reason, which is as inexplicable today as it was then, Crown International picked it up. No one saw the film, but it really helped Kevin's career. In subsequent years Kevin and Jim became partners, started their own company, and that was the company that produced *Dances with Wolves*.

My problems to this day with *Stacy's Knights,* insofar as I think about them, all have to do with the movie's production values and casting and things like that. As far as the screenplay's concerned, I think I'm pretty pleased with it. Sure, I'd probably like to have a little more background and back story on certain characters, and I might like to see things develop a little differently, but it's the same old writer's lament: Once you turn in your script and make the final adjustments on it and people go out to shoot it, it's pretty much out of your control.

Now, as it turned out, that wasn't necessarily the case with *Dances with Wolves*. With the exception of a few improvisational moments, it was shot basically as written, which is something of a gigantic miracle in itself. My first draft, I believe, was about 150 pages, with the shooting script somewhere around the mid-130s, which means there are a lot of long cinematic moments, since the movie lasted three hours. For instance, the buffalo hunt is probably half a page in the script but lasts several minutes at least on-screen. I think that's one of the great legacies of *Dances*. It proved that if you had the right kind of movie and you did it in a way that fully absorbed the audience, you could stretch what was considered to be the limits of people's viewing attention; it gave movies a lot more latitude. The powers that be felt that people could endure more, so the next several years, and even today, there are a lot of big movies that last three hours.

A lot of people come home from the movies and sit around the kitchen table and say to themselves that they could do better than that, and that's when they start a screenplay. Most of the time, though, they drop out; and they drop out because they totally underestimate the degree of difficulty. Either that or they've deluded themselves into thinking that what they've written really works, when in fact they've had no experience or seasoning or any real commitment. You know, the general public looks at the artist or creative person as someone who's kind of having fun and think that it's really not so difficult, it's not as hard as punching a clock in a factory every day, and it's something that could be done with a relatively small amount of labor. People think that writing is something they'd do if they only had the time. They really have no idea how hard it is to keep your ass in that seat for hours.

Me, I call it "sitting in the chair," because I write everything longhand. It's very much against my nature to be so sedentary, so I've had to discipline myself to a very high degree over the years just to sit in the chair and kind of dream myself away from all of the things in the modern world that are distracting and into some kind of place where wonderful things can happen. Being able to do that over a long period of time is really a marathon run. You have to find a way to keep your passion alive through all of that time. My last novel, the sequel to *Dances,* is a very good example. I prepared to write that book for eleven years, and when I finally sat down to write it my wife was pregnant with our third child. We had to do a major move and go through the final stages of pregnancy and delivery and birth, all with two other young children needing care and attention all the time. It was during that time that I wrote *The Holy Road.* And you know, sometimes I look back on it and I'm not sure I know exactly how I did that, but there's some kind of spirit that I just tap into that sustains me through it all.

I don't ever start out on something unless I really feel that it has a good shot to sustain me through whatever else might be going on, like all that stuff I just mentioned. I think the choice of the material itself is probably the first and the most critical component. It's very similar to choosing a mate. If you choose a mate that you really feel you can sustain life with over a long period of time, and you make the right choice there, your chances for a successful marriage are quite good. If that choice is made rashly or if it's made on a bad-hair day or a good-hair day, it could be trouble. But the choice of material is the first and most critical element in any writing project for me.

My daily process has changed over the years, just like a painter's or musician's in the studio would: The more experience you have, the more adjustments you make. When I first started out, I would keep copious note cards and produce outlines on butcher paper that I'd hang all over the walls. Today, I don't do any of that; I simply follow my nose through the whole process and trust that the commitment I've made, and the material that I've chosen, will carry me through. It's almost like an athletic endeavor to me. If I miss two or three days, I find myself struggling a little bit—just the way an athlete does if he misses his regular workout. I try to avoid that, but delays and lapses are unavoidable, so what I bet on now is my experience and my discipline. My wife can tell you that I'm a bit difficult to live with if I'm not writing regularly. My best hours for work used to be nighttime, but I have three children under five, so now it's morning.

Pretty much as soon as I hit the chair, I'm working. First thing I do is crank up the music—it's absolutely critical to my process—as loud as I can, to the point where it's overwhelming and shuts out all other distractions. I also use marijuana frequently as a way to focus myself. I don't know whether I'm clinically addicted or not, but I think for me marijuana really enhances my ability to focus and my ability to concentrate on the task at hand. If I omitted that, I wouldn't be telling the whole truth. Marijuana is one of the tools that I use. Music is another.

The music is like a wave that I'm bodysurfing. You don't really think about the wave when you're bodysurfing; you think about the position of your body and the beach up ahead. So the music is pushing me along, and very often when I'm really in a groove, which is most of the time, the music is just something that is kind of in my bloodstream. I don't know how else to describe it. I can go through a whole record and the record will end and I will be barely aware that it was on. The pen has been churning all the while.

If you look at my manuscripts, you'll see that I not only edit as I go, but I also try to spend some time every day going over the previous day's work and catching the wretched excesses. I never catch them all, but I do a lot of editing before I ever even have a typed manuscript spit out to work on more.

Maybe I should tell you how *Dances with Wolves* got written in the first place. At the time, in 1986, when I began it, I had to make a choice: Was I going to write a book, or was I going to continue to pay the rent? I chose the book. If I had taken a job to pay the rent, I would never have written the book, because I wouldn't have had time. So I gave notice at my abode and stored stuff in my friends' houses around Los Angeles, put some stuff in the trunk of my 1970 Chrysler, and drove around town until December, crashing at people's houses, occasionally sleeping in the car, watching people's places while they were on vacation or whatever—and all that time I was writing the book in artist's unlined sketch books. When I was finished, I typed it myself. In all, I probably lived three or four days at a time at forty or fifty different places.

I was in my forties and had never really made any money from writing, only enough to keep me alive long enough to write some more. But when I finished *Dances with Wolves,* I felt that I'd done something important—

achieved something—on the terms that I set out to meet. Still, I had no agent, no publisher, no money. I borrowed $1,000 from Laura Ziskin, the only person I knew with money, and basically exiled myself from Los Angeles, because I could not face my friends anymore; I'd been freeloading for the better part of a year and I just didn't want to live like that. So I put my little puppy and my stuff in the car, and just started driving east, thinking very strongly that I would never be successful as a writer. Really, I had made every effort that I could to penetrate Hollywood, and that hadn't worked. And now I'd written a book that no one would read, even in manuscript, and I wondered what the point was of doing this anymore. I decided to get to a place where I could kind of reorganize myself and maybe get a job working with horses. There were always horses around when I was growing up, and I love horses. I felt that if I was going to devote myself to something, horses were better than anything else.

You know, no one likes to give up the ghost; no one likes to admit defeat. I hated what was happening, but I was determined to get something out of my life. Hollywood had become a very alien world to me. I didn't feel like I fit in there, didn't feel that I would ever get anywhere there. And getting the book published—well, I was hopeful, but didn't have any illusions about that either. I just thought I had written a really good book—had given it my all—and if that wasn't good enough, well . . .

There sat the typed manuscript, in a box in the trunk, next to my dirty clothes. At that point, no one had really read it. Actually, Jim Wilson had, and thought it was very

very good, and when I left town he was trying to get someone at the William Morris Agency to read it, because that
was Kevin's agency at the time. But they said they didn't
read stuff like that. In fact, Jim was also trying to get
Kevin to read it, and Kevin refused. I found out later, and
I don't know whether this is true, that the reason Kevin
didn't want to read it was that he was afraid he would
like it, and if he liked it, he'd have to try to get it made,
and trying to get it made would be impossible—and he
didn't want to set himself up for that. Which explains,
true or not, why he resisted reading it for quite some time.

Anyway, Jim pestered William Morris for a very long
time. And finally, to get rid of him, someone there said,
"Look, we'll have our head reader read it, and she'll give
you some feedback." Well, she read it and said it was a
wonderful book, that William Morris should be repre-
senting it, and she recommended that it go to their literary
office in New York. Which it did. And then I got a call
that they wanted to represent it. Unfortunately, it was rejected by every hardcover publisher in New York. It finally
found a home with Fawcett Gold Medal Paperbacks,
which released it in 1988 as the kind of book they perceived it to be—a romance novel. Kevin finally read it and
was obviously knocked out by it.

When he called me, I was in my rathole rented room in
Bisbee, Arizona, a little town just above the Mexican bor-
der, east of Nogales. Two days before I'd been fired from
my job as a dishwasher at the China Land Chinese Cuisine
restaurant. It's pretty funny to think they even had a Chinese restaurant in a town like that, which probably didn't

even have a doctor. I'd been fired for asking for a new pair of dishwashing gloves, because the old ones had holes in them and my hands were getting scalded, and I was making $3.35 an hour for a split shift, and the owner said I should buy my own gloves, and I said, "How can I buy my own gloves, when you're paying me three bucks an hour?" and she said, "Well, you're not a very good dishwasher anyway," and fired me. So there I was sitting in my room when the phone rings, and it's Kevin, asking if I'd come back to Hollywood and write a screenplay based on the novel. And I said, "I'll be there tomorrow."

I drove straight to his house and stayed there for a few days. I can't recall where he and Jim got the seed money for me to start the screenplay, but of course it was a king's ransom to me at the time. It was enough to get a little place in Silver Lake, a postage stamp–sized place. That's where I wrote most of the screenplay—in longhand.

From the beginning, I made a conscious decision to not look at the book, figuring that the book was already there and this was something new. I think probably the biggest difficulty that a novelist-screenwriter has in separating from his novel to write the screenplay is accepting the fact that the twain do not meet. Anyway, I wrote the first draft and delivered it to Kevin and Jim, and Kevin came back and pointed to a bunch of stuff in the book and said, "Look, this isn't there, and this isn't there, and this isn't there—we've gotta get it all in." And I said, "But it's already a hundred and fifty pages and it's only going to get bigger," and he said, "No, it's got to be smaller, but we can still get all this stuff in." So I started working on the second of about six drafts.

At one point Kevin and Jim took the draft to Nelson Entertainment, a British company that was a big deal at that time, and the executives there came back and said, "Look, we'll make the movie if you change Stands with a Fist to an Indian woman who's been repatriated after being captured by white people." And I said, "What's the point of that?" And Jim and Kevin said, "Well, we're not sure, but the Nelson guys said they were inclined to make the movie if we make the changes." That's when Jim and Kevin looked me right in the eye and said, "If you don't do it, we'll get someone else to do it." And they also warned me not to ask for too much money to redo it. So I went home and searched my soul and realized probably the wisest route would be to stay involved. So I went ahead and did it to the best of my ability. But no one was really enthusiastic about it so we went back to the original. I'd say that the sixth draft of *Dances* looked very much like the first, but it's a process you have to go through, and it's a war of attrition for the writer, because you have to deal with all these people who are coming at you, telling you what the magic bullet is to make a successful movie. If you hang in there and run the gauntlet, your chances, I think, are better than if you don't.

The way I analyze notes is, if there's a repetitive theme in them, from a variety of sources, all hitting on the same thing, I'll be inclined to take a crack at that. But if it doesn't add anything, and if it's not well thought out, I ignore it. I do like to think that I'm open to any good idea, though. I've probably been typed in Hollywood as someone who's far too expensive and far too intractable to do movies, and I've basically been shut out of Hollywood for the last four years. That's all going to change with *The Holy Road,* which is being done overseas.

It's funny, because for a few years after the Oscar, people were willing to have me write "all work and no play makes Jack a dull boy" for high amounts of money. I've always been the first person to raise his hand if someone's got a better idea. Of course I'm passionate about the work, and of course I'm going to fight for my point of view, because I feel like I'm the one who's put all the work into it. But really, if someone has a better idea, I've always been more than willing to adapt.

Part of the problem—and it's probably worse now than it's ever been—is that people don't read; they don't like to read. And particularly they don't like to read screenplays. What happens is that, in Hollywood, people usually go into a screenplay expecting to be disappointed, because the quality of writing or the conceptualizing just doesn't fit the bill for them, and after reading hundreds of them, the last thing a person wants to do is pick up a screenplay that is so lamentable. So if they do read at all, they like to read in shorthand; what they like to see are bullet points—stuff that is the complete opposite of a world created out of written words. They don't feel like they have the time, the energy, or the desire to access that kind of world. They want to read, "This is a movie about King Kong meeting Bambi, and there's a happy ending." That's the way a lot of these things are based.

It's a curious relationship that Hollywood and New York have—movies and publishing. There can be these incredible bidding wars over an article that appears in the

Sunday *New York Times Magazine* or over a book that's coming from a best-selling novelist. I guess what's in vogue now is pushing the edge of everything—storm edge books, mountain-climbing books, survival books. New York generally gets to these things first, with magazine articles and books. Most of it gets optioned for movies, and some of it actually gets made, and by then New York's already on to the next big thing.

For me personally, the big danger in adapting a book to the screen is being too close to the book—not being able to make the leap from something that's intensely literate to something that's intensely cinematic. If you live in a literate world and you're not steeped in a cinematic world, I think the process is filled with all kinds of dangers: You can't quite make the leap to something that's almost exclusively visual. What's necessary in adapting a screenplay is disengaging from the world of literature and engaging in the world of visual elements. I can give you an example with the new book, which has some events in it that cannot be shot any other way than as special effects. Although they're grounded in real experience, they have to be rendered in a special-effect kind of way—and you know what? That's really fortuitous for me, because it starts right away to give me a more cinematic sense that I hope will transfer to a lot of the things that I do in the writing of the screenplay. That's not to say that *The Holy Road* as a movie is going to be laden with special effects; it's not. But it creates a kind of environment that allows me to start thinking in broader, cinematic images, and it helps me to find a way to render scenes and sequences visually. Basically it's the difference between writing a scene in a book in which someone's standing on a beach looking at a tidal wave, and writing that scene in a movie. In the book, you're writing about the character and all of the things that are going through the character's head as the tidal wave approaches. Well, in a movie, you've got to pretty much forget about that; you have to find a way to let that moment when the character faces the tsunami show on the screen by describing some action or reaction that describes what's inside his head. It may be subtle or it may not, but it's the only thing that counts in a movie.

Of course, in *Dances with Wolves* the movie, we had a voice-over narrator, the main character, letting us know what he thought. But it couldn't be used in every scene, and you wouldn't want it to be. Think of the scene when Dunbar dances around the fire. It was a good scene in the book, I think, and it was a good scene in the movie. In the book I spent a fair amount of time talking about his feelings as he was dancing, and in the movie I thought Kevin really pulled out something there because as an actor he made a commitment to sort of go all the way with that dancing around the fire, and the way he did it spoke volumes about what he was feeling. If there had been a voice-over right then, the whole feeling would have been destroyed.

I'm a fourth-generation published writer. Books were always respected around my house. My great-grandfather, J. Y. F. Blake, wrote a book published around the turn of the century called *A West Pointer with the Boers,* an account of his service in the Boer War. My grandfather, Aldridge Blake, wrote political books. And my uncle, Forrester Blake, wrote historical novels in the forties and fifties. I think it's too much to say directly that I wanted to follow in their footsteps, but I did want to be a writer. My family was very fractured. It had all of the classic ruptures and divorces and all of that kind of stuff. So it wasn't what you would call a tight-knit family at all, and I viewed all of these people pretty much at a distance. Still, I guess I felt some kind of metaphysical kinship with them, because when I was a little kid and I stayed home sick from school, I would usually write stories and make drawings to illustrate them. That was something that came naturally to me, and so many other fields held no interest for me at all. The idea of being a grown-up in the dull, colorless fifties didn't have much appeal; the only signs of life I saw were Little Richard and Elvis. When it came time for me to actually start doing something, I gravitated toward journalism, which was a way to access writing. I didn't start out thinking I was going to be a novelist or a screenwriter. I wanted to do journalism and I got involved in that in the Air Force, and then in college to a very deep degree. Then I dropped out of school in my senior year and came out to Los Angeles and started freelancing for alternative news services and things like that. I got on as an associate editor at the *LA Free Press* and did basically underground journalism for several years.

I tired of journalism because of its transience. I wanted to do something that could maybe last a bit longer. I'd already tried to write a little bit of fiction and had been totally rejected. Well, it came to me that in college I'd loved going to small art-house cinemas, and I thought that what I should be doing was writing movies. So eventually I ended up in the Bay Area at a film program Antioch College was running up there. It's not that I wanted to be a filmmaker; I just wanted to know how it worked—how you can figure out foot-candles and how you can do hot-splicing and how you can run a 16-mm camera and load it; things like that. I figured all that would give me some kind of basis for understanding how movies actually worked. I felt that if I knew that, then it would help me with writing. And I think it has. Anyway, that's where I met Jim. And the rest is history.

JOHN IRVING

I've admired John Irving's writing since reading *The World According to Garp* in 1978. He is an old-fashioned literary novelist whose books are worlds unto themselves. I began the interview by noting that I couldn't think of another writer in his stratum who'd successfully written a screenplay.

JAMES SALTER IS A WONDERFUL NOVELIST AND HE WROTE *Downhill Racer,* but I suppose that point has been made. The reason probably has something to do with the nature of writing and why someone chooses to write fiction in the first place. My guess is that a novelist who isn't very highly regarded, or even one who is but who's struggling to make a living writing, might have all kinds of reasons to be interested in writing screenplays—a paycheck, for one thing. But when one thinks about a novelist who at least makes a living by writing novels, or whose work is well enough known or regarded so that his or her life as a novelist is comfortable, the reasons are fewer. Someone in those circumstances—myself included, by the way—has very little incentive to write and try to sell a screenplay or put himself in the hands of, well, merciless collaborators; or involve himself in the process of storytelling by committee. You just don't want to do that when you enjoy the luxury of staying at home and writing and not having a gun to your head about deadlines; and furthermore you get to decide yourself which of your words and ideas will be kept in the text. Because despite the protestations of editors and copy editors, you don't have to change a period if you don't want to. That's a pretty unassailable position to give up when you compare it to confronting the suggestions, or even the orders, of countless others.

That's the devil's advocacy point of view. And I learned it the hard way, through experience, with my first novel, *Setting Free the Bears,* which was published in 1969. Columbia Pictures bought the screen rights, which I was stupid enough to sell with no right of approval or ownership. I worked with the director Irvin Kershner on the screenplay. He's a very nice man, a talented man; we're still good friends, and I look back at that time with great fondness. But the experience came to naught, and did so in a typically ugly and undermining fashion, with alleged checks "being in the mail" or just plain late.

Anyway, from that experience I wondered very strongly why anyone who wants to be a writer would subject himself to that—that is, if he didn't have to. And I'm not referring to the collaboration with Kershner; I'm referring to what was done to both him and to me and to that script at the hands of others, and to how manipulated I think we both felt. Which is why, on later books, when directors whom I much admired, like George Hill and Tony Richardson, wanted to make *The World According to Garp* and *Hotel New Hampshire,* I was so happy to say, "Gee, you go ahead and do it. I don't want anything to do with it." The funny thing is that George wanted me to write the screenplay for *Garp,* while Tony wanted to write the *New Hampshire* screenplay himself and was actually relieved when I said I didn't want to do it. I kept my distance, because I never was and am still not a writer who believes that a novel is in any way incomplete if a film isn't made from it. Nor do I feel that a good novel is in any way tarnished if a not-very-good film is made from it. People who see a bad film and feel they know the book, or for that matter see a good one and feel they know the book, are, well, not readers in the first place.

Now, all of that said, let me get to why I *did* write the screenplay for *The Cider House Rules* and see it through to the end. There were two elements at play in this project that I'm frankly not sure will ever be at play to quite this degree in my career again. The first and probably most important was that this was the only novel of mine that I actually envisioned as a film while writing it. Even as I was writing *Cider House* in the first draft, I could see a film in it. However complex and long a novel it was, it did have a kind of symmetry that most of my novels don't. It's a story about a kid who thinks he's unlucky—he's born in the wrong place and wants to get out of where he comes from; but, unbeknownst to him, he belongs there more deeply than he imagines. That's where the symmetry comes in: The story ends up back where it began, which makes it much more adaptable as a film.

As I was writing that book I saw the main character, Homer Wells, stepping off that train and returning to the orphanage—saw it as though watching a film. I knew that was the emotional ending and it was a very visual one. I believe I knew what it would feel like to the audience, to see that young man coming back to where he belongs. For years the first chapter of that book, "The Boy Who Belonged to St. Cloud's," was also the working title for the novel. That distinguished *Cider House* among my ten novels. So it wasn't a question of somebody coming to me and saying, "Would you like a crack at this screenplay?" and my saying, "No thanks, I have my day job and I like it better." It was something that was already an idea in my mind even before I finished the book. All of which made it difficult to say no when Phillip Borsos, the first director to involve himself in *Cider House,* approached me about making a film. I was able to put aside my less satisfying experiences on the other films made of my books, and to decide that I'd better treat the screenplay the way I treat the writing of a novel; which is to say that I would have every approval—script approval, director approval, cast approval—or I wouldn't go ahead.

A number of friends in the business told me that I didn't have a chance of getting the film made that way. To which I said, "Fine." But Phillip, bless his heart, subscribed to my vision. He said, "Okay, we're partners. Every creative decision is going to be yours and mine, and any third party is going to have to subscribe to that letter of agreement between us." Well, of course, no one did. They tried to jerk him around in unmerciful ways and the poor guy died at the age of forty-two. Then Richard Gladstein approached me. I said, "Look, this is an experiment. I've let books go and let other people make them, and I've not been interested in the process and may never be interested in the process again. But in this case I see how to do it." And he went to Miramax, and Miramax said, "Fine." And then we went out and looked for directors, and tried a couple before we got to Lasse Hallström.

I'd actually seen Lasse's film *My Life as a Dog* when Phillip Borsos was still alive; we'd both agreed that Lasse would do a good job with *Cider House*. From the very first meeting, Lasse and Richard and I were on the same page. We agreed that we'd talk about all the creative decisions regarding cast, script, and cutting, and that if one of the three felt strongly opposed to what the other two wanted, the other two would find another way to go. This wasn't majority rule. Strangely, as it turned out, there never was an issue that one of us felt so strongly about that we had to say to the other two, "I can't go there."

Lasse and I are well suited to each other. His Europeaness as a director suits my old-fashionedness as a narrative writer of, as someone described to me, nineteenth-century novels. Lasse lets the camera linger. He goes slowly. And as a consequence, a two-hour film by Lasse Hallström feels, by today's jumpy standards, longer than a two-and-a-half-hour film by somebody who cuts frenetically in and out of scenes. *The Cider House Rules* isn't a film that tries to capture the audience's attention through motion.

Now, there's one other aspect here of my new appreciation of the screenplay form, at least as it regards me and my novels. The fact is, my day job is principally solitary. I spend between three and a half and five and a half years writing a story that nobody but me sees. I read parts of it aloud to my wife, and I have an assistant who transcribes first drafts and cleans things up so that he or she knows what I'm doing, but I don't share the writing process with anybody—and I like that. That is my principal creative endeavor; it's a solitary one.

At the same time I'd have to say that it's been such a thrill for me, at age fifty-nine, to have the opportunity for a second career. No, I'd never trade writing a novel for writing screenplays, but the opportunity to write screenplays now with these collaborators that I know I work well with and like is a wonderful thing. It's gratifying at my age to discover this other thing that you can do between novels, or when you have a novel that's at the note-taking stage. It's great to be able to have a collaborative side of your life when the main thrust of it is so much alone.

I'd have to say, too, that the experience of writing *Cider House* has confirmed what I've always believed as a writer, that the most important and essential element of writing is rewriting. My sense of things is that the first drafts of my novels are no better than anybody else's, but I believe that I have a capacity for revisiting a book over and over again, and that capacity may be a little greater than some other writers'. I believe in revision.

When I turn in the manuscript, I listen to what my editor has to say. I want a strong editor, one with strong opinions and skills, and I've been lucky enough in my career to have always had one. That doesn't mean I'll do everything he or she suggests.

I guess this has to do with Lasse in the sense that my relationships with editors over the years have prepared me to really listen to people. Yes, maybe I'll act upon only two-fifths or less of the suggestions an editor makes, but I really want that editor to make those suggestions. Same with the director. Same with the producer, Richard. He's very good at notes for a script.

I'll tell you something else. One of my favorite parts of the whole filmmaking process turned out to be similar to one of my favorite parts of the novel-writing process. I really loved the editing process and shaving the whole thing down from two hours and twenty, to two hours and fourteen, to two hours and four minutes. I came out of that experience feeling that you can never rewrite enough. If you're feeling tired of the project, well then you step away from it until you're not tired of it. Frankly, this last novel that I've just completed benefited from the script-writing and -editing experience, because I kept feeling I could go over the manuscript two more times instead of one more time; I could proofread the galleys four times instead of three times, and so on. It was very much like Richard and Lasse and I going over that script and one of us saying, "Hey, what about that? What about that scene we took out? Suppose we put that here and move this . . . ?"

Now, it occurs to me that another reason there may be

so few novelists adapting their own screenplays with any success is that, quite possibly, the novelist may be the worst person to adapt his own work if the work is big and sprawling with hundreds of pages of incidents and dozens of characters that could never be used in any film. Writing a successful adaptation means re-imagining the work. I'll give you an example from *Cider House*. Near the beginning of the book a couple named the Winkles tries to adopt little Homer but they're killed in a tragic and comical scene that seems inherently cinematic but which we just couldn't fit into the movie because, for one thing, we needed to get to the grown-up Homer as quickly as possible. In fact, that's why we did away with most of the first third of the book and left a lot of very wonderful scenes behind, as well as some vibrant characters, many of whom became composite characters in the movie. I'm also thinking of a scene from the book in which the young Homer sleeps with an adoptive family's daughter. It's a funny scene and a good scene, but we all felt that it established too comedic a tone.

Many of the decisions about what to keep and what to lose had less to do with drama than with the realities of filmmaking. The way things work, you've got to have your star up on the screen most of the time. My sense is that films fail at the passage of time when they have a child actor up there for twenty minutes, and then that actor is gone and replaced by the star—in this case Tobey Maguire. That tends not to work in a movie the way it does in a book. In a book you build affection for a character from whatever age he begins on the page, and the reader carries that affection forward. But in a movie, you're not seeing this character in your mind's eye and being carried along as he grows. You're seeing the character just suddenly show up; he really doesn't bring with him any affection, because the viewer's eye sees a different actor than the child grown into an adult. Knowing that, my instinct was to show Homer's childhood all through photographs during the title sequence, and from the moment the credits end there would be Tobey, lifting the lid of that operating room pail, and by his expression we'd know what's in it. That's where I wanted to go with it. Lasse greatly improved on this static idea. And to compensate for what was lost, I created some characters who hadn't been in the book. The Buster character, for example, was a very important character in the film, who for me replaced the figure of Homer as an innocent boy in the book.

One thing I'd like to emphasize is that any screenwriter who's credited with writing a good screenplay almost certainly has a terrific director, as well as actors who've made the film look as good as it does. The truth is, if you don't have those things then nobody's going to notice whether the screenplay's any good or not. It's no surprise that the screenplays nominated for Oscars in both the original and adapted categories are going to be from pretty good films. I really fed off those sessions with Lasse and Richard, and I have to say that I really enjoyed not being, for once, the only one thinking about what could happen next or what the hell was going to replace this scene, if we had to lose it. You don't get into that kind of situation in a novel, because if the scenes are good, you don't lose them; you keep them all. In a novel, the only questions a novelist has to answer are whether something's good and advances the story, and whether anybody is going to lose interest. You don't care if it turns out to be a 725-page novel or a 525-page novel—but we all cared that this not be an overlong film.

So much of a good screenplay is really not even in the screenplay; it's in the performances, and letting the camera work just enough to capture them. I remember Lasse's instructing me how he wanted me to create certain scenes in order to give him options, so that if the actors were good enough, the camera could find a way to communicate something important about the characters and story without dialogue—something that's subtextual and rich. For instance, there are major passages in the book in which Homer reads Dickens aloud. They're meant to have a dramatic richness about them that explains a great many things about Homer. Well, those scenes couldn't possibly have been in the movie, because you don't make movies about characters reading to other characters for half an hour at a time. But what Lasse did, in the one scene where Homer reads to the young orphans, is pan over the faces of the children. Their faces are so expressive that the viewer ends up getting what the reader was intended to get from Homer's reading in the book—only you learn something about all the characters, not just Homer.

To get back to the question of why more literary novelists either don't write screenplays or haven't often succeeded at it, I'll give you another example of how novel-writing and screenwriting are different disciplines.

In the novel *The Cider House Rules,* I had two characters, Wally and Candy, a young couple about whom you knew a great deal before they ever arrived at the orphanage. And when they get there, you know they're reluctantly, painfully there for an abortion. In the movie, the first time the viewer sees them, they've already arrived at the orphanage and all the orphans are crowding around, seeing them as potential parents; and because of the way they interact with the orphans, the viewers may actually believe that they're there to adopt a child. So in just a few moments, we've gained a great deal of information about these two people. It was just a short scene—an image, really—that's worth a thousand or more words. But the passion and proclivity of the literary novelist is words; letting the camera tell the story is perhaps counterintuitive to him.

In the novel of *Cider House,* it's also quite clear that Homer is in love with Candy—so there were choices to be made there, as well. Was this movie going to be a love story? Looking at the three main stories, the Homer-Candy-Wally story, the story of the black fruit pickers, and the relationship between Homer and Dr. Larch, the love story seemed least important to me. More important were those black migrants and what Homer learned from them—the cider-house experience itself—and the all-important relationship with Larch. Something had to give, and it was the love story. What we decided to do was, first, to get Wally in and out of the story so quickly so that he and Homer could not be the best of friends; we didn't have time to make them friends and also didn't want to compromise the audience's sympathy with Homer by making him betray anything remotely resembling a best friend. Second, we decided to let Homer play younger and more innocent than he is in the novel, and also to make Candy a kind of older, more knowledgeable, and less likable woman than she is in the novel; she becomes a little harder, more flirtatious, more of an instigator of the relationship that develops between her and Homer. That accounts for why we cast Charlize Theron, because we were looking for someone who not only seemed a cut more sophisticated than Tobey, but who also looked older and bigger.

The aspect of the movie I worried about most was the passage of time, which I mentioned earlier. It was so important to have an emotional impact when Homer returns, and originally I thought that was going to be lost, because in the film he's been away only eighteen months (rather than fifteen years). I agonized over how we would compensate for that. And it wasn't until I met the kids, that first day on the set, that I realized we were actually going to gain something, not lose it. Because when Homer comes back to the orphanage after only a year and a half, he comes back to the same kids who were there when he left; nobody's adopted them. So not only do we have a reunion of sorts, but we also get to make the point, which I made often in the novel, that kids in this situation don't all get adopted. Most of them, in fact, stay there until they get as old as Homer. Now, in this structure, we got to make both points, and the resolution of the story was richer for it emotionally. To see Homer again through the eyes of those children—not just through the eyes of those old nurses who never expected to see him again—was a wonderful bonus that we hadn't counted on.

I also learned that fifteen years in a book is not fifteen years in a movie. A movie operates on its own time, so to convey the passage of it, all you have to do is keep him away from the orphanage for sixty or seventy minutes; an hour of cinema time could very well be fifteen years in real time. Cinema time is what people sitting in a movie theater relate to.

I think it would be instructive to point out something else we did that seemed radical at the time but which in retrospect comes out well. In the novel Homer is partially motivated to leave the orphanage by Fuzzy's death, which he's been powerless to stop. Larch's failure to keep Fuzzy alive—medicine's failure—intrudes into young Homer's life as powerfully as the conflict over abortion does. And in the novel, it is Homer who feels Fuzzy's death most keenly. But we recognized that we already had all the opportunity in the world to make Homer a sensitive and feeling character; we weren't worried about the audience's losing sympathy for Homer if he wasn't the one feeling distraught for Fuzzy. What we did worry about was giving enough to Dr. Larch. We were going to be away from him for a long time, after Homer leaves the orphanage, and we worried that this role would seem too thin, even by supporting-actor standards; and we knew the audience would wonder where Michael Caine was all that time. What I did, therefore, was make Dr. Larch the one who feels Fuzzy's death most keenly; I kept Fuzzy in the film as long as I could, after Homer leaves, instead of having him die *before* Homer leaves. In that way we gave Dr. Larch an emotional pitch that keeps him very much alive in the audience's mind, even though we're mostly away from him in the middle part of the film. I turned Fuzzy into a kind of confidant. It's Fuzzy who asks Dr. Larch if he ever knew who his mother was. It's Larch who arranges a private screening of *King Kong* for Fuzzy. It's Larch who's there when he dies. And then it's Homer's counterpart, the Buster character, who represents what it must have been like for Homer to be a kid there. It's he, not Homer, who has to lie and tell the kids that Fuzzy's been adopted.

One of the things we lost from the book to the movie, and you can imagine the conversation about it, is when Homer cleans up the operating room after Candy's abortion. In the novel, he sees her pubic hair—a blond hair that he holds up to the light—because she's been shaved. Well, he keeps it in his wallet—and for the longest time we kept that in the script. For some tortured reason he was going to open his wallet when they get to the drive-in movie, and she's going to recognize her pubic hair! Richard did not want to lose the scene, but Lasse and I kept saying, "I don't think this is going to go. How do we do pubic hair?" So we kept taking it out and then we'd have a meeting and somebody would look a little depressed and either Richard or Lasse would say, "I think we should put the pubic hair back in." Finally, thank God, we had the sense to keep it out. It never would have worked.

Believe me, there were any number of scenes in the book

that I, as the novelist, thought were both interesting and cinematic but which we couldn't keep. In particular there's a scene having to do with Mr. Rose's vomiting on the ferris wheel, which has a strong metaphorical significance in the book. We had to lose it, because we did not want to lose a moment of Michael Caine and did not want to lose a minute of conflict between Tobey and Michael. Every time we looked at those other elements and knew that it would take at least ten minutes to set up the ferris wheel, we knew it didn't belong in the movie.

Interestingly, decisions like that also made the issue of race and race relations much more subtextual in the movie than they were in the book. In fact, they changed the whole focus of the book. In the novel, Dr. Larch is the dominant character; in the film, Homer is. But I really can't say that either Dr. Larch or Mr. Rose were given short shrift in the movie—other characters, yes, but not those two; I don't think they were compromised. Which is a fascinating conclusion to reach for the writer who gave them all life in the first place. I suggest you take a look at the DVD of *Cider House Rules,* because one of the tracks on it has outtakes and unused scenes, one of which is a long operating room scene with Michael and Tobey that got left on the floor because there was no way to cut it; it was so appreciably longer than the scenes surrounding it that undue significance attached itself to it. There's also a scene on the roof with the black guys looking up at the stars; we couldn't use that because of cinematographic problems. There's also a rather genial sort of introductory scene, in which Mr. Rose introduces Homer to all the other pickers by name, that was absolutely delightful but too leisurely, given that this is a point in the story where Homer has come to a new place and you just don't want the narrative to slow down. All three are fabulous scenes that were painful to lose. The point, I suppose, is that I learned so much about screenwriting by actually having a hand in making the film and seeing what other kinds of considerations must be given that process. It gave me a greater appreciation not only for movies and writing them, but also for novels and the writing of them. So many things go into the making of the movie, whereas only the novelist's brain and talent and ambition go into the novel. It's an interesting contrast.

TOM SCHULMAN

Tom and I met one morning in a conference room at the head-
quarters of the Writers Guild of America (he's active in the Guild
and Guild Foundation), where negotiations would soon be held regarding a possible strike (which thanks to him and others did not
take place). My first question was, "How does one reconcile the
writer of *Dead Poets Society* with the writer of *Honey, I Shrunk the
Kids*?"

AND DON'T FORGET *8 HEADS IN A DUFFEL BAG*. THE AN-
swer, I suppose, is that I like all kinds of movies. *Dead
Poets Society* was an original; *Honey, I Shrunk the Kids*
was a rewrite of someone else's original. Maybe the
themes are similar; I don't know, I haven't really been able
to look at all my own work and isolate a consistent or
coherent theme. Somebody once said, "I write to find out
what I think." That's me. What attracted me to *Honey*
was that the idea of kids being shrunk reminded me of
what it felt like to be a kid—small, powerless, at the mercy
of grown-ups.

Everything I write is autobiographical in the sense that I shape characters only from the people I know in my life. They start out as people I know and then they change as the story changes them. *Dead Poets* started out actually as a script about an acting school I was in. After a while it just started to feel like the whole venture was just sort of inbred—a Hollywood kind of story. So I threw that idea out, but what remained was the notion of a teacher who inspires kids, and the idea that one of the characters wants to become an actor. I was enjoying using a teacher as a sort of mouthpiece for ideas, which got me thinking about other experiences I'd had with inspirational teachers. But first I needed an antagonist and a conflict.

I thought back to my time at Montgomery Bell Academy in Nashville. It was a day school and much more liberal than the school portrayed in *Dead Poets,* but it did have a headmaster who wished he could take the school back to the days of more traditional boarding schools. The sixties were closing in and he was desperate to hold on to some traditions. So I had a sense of what that school might have been like had he been able to exert his will on it, and it seemed like a good conflict to pit a wonderful teacher who wants to fight tradition against that headmaster. I set the movie in 1959. The last year of the fifties, the decade of conformity.

That overall theme of creativity and nonconformity really came directly from my life and my own struggle. To write the movie, I put myself in the position of a teacher who's trying to communicate his ideas to students in as engaging and entertaining a way as possible—not because he's showing off but because he wants them to get it. Writing this script was a kind of voyage of self discovery for me. I got it off my chest and moved on— not that I've necessarily abandoned any of the ideas that I was working on in that movie, but I've grown a little since then and when I look back on some of the ideas and themes in that movie, I question whether I still agree with my arguments there. I think the notion of rebellion is perhaps more complicated, less black and white, than the way I depicted it in that movie. Can you tell I've since become a parent?

Peter Weir, the director of *Dead Poets*, went to a boarding school that was very conservative. He told me that sometimes he looked back on those days and felt they weren't so bad. I guess the bottom line is that wherever you can learn discipline is a good place, because it takes self-discipline to succeed in life. Then, too, it's sometimes not such a bad thing to feel as though you're an outsider, that you don't fit in—especially if you're going to be a writer.

Anyway, the movie probably has its deepest roots in my childhood. I grew up in the South, and we were Jewish. Jews there and then were under heavy pressure to assimilate. There was always that feeling of being an outsider, of being different and having to prove yourself in some way. In the school I went to, there were maybe twelve Jewish guys out of five hundred kids. I remember opening the door on the first day to go outside and seeing this rather fat Jewish kid lying in the stairwell and a bunch of guys were tossing pennies at him. He was playing the clown for them, trying to scarf up the pennies—playing "Jew" for these Gentile boys. They were all laughing, and he was laughing too, but it was a grotesque kind of indicator of what those guys really thought of us.

There were clubs and fraternities that actually excluded Jews. The biggest club in the school was the Young Men's Christian Society. Every three weeks they'd have a meeting, and 490 kids would be there—everybody in the school but us 12 Jews, who'd sit and wait for it to end in study hall. It took a tremendous effort on my part to sort of deny and avoid any feelings of being left out while at the same time wanting to be a part of it all. I didn't understand why I couldn't be.

I remember being seven or so, horsing around during the breaks in Saturday religious school. A bunch of us went downstairs where we weren't supposed to go, into the basement of the temple, and opened the door to a room where there sat large blowups of pictures from the Holocaust that were going to be used for a lecture to the adults. These photos were the most horrifying things you could imagine—trenches full of corpses, ghastly. The six of us who found them were devastated. We didn't know anything at that age about the Holocaust. Well, the rabbi took us up into his office and all of us were really upset and one of us asked the rabbi to tell us what these pictures were. He told us, and then someone said, "Rabbi, how can there be a God if this happened?" And the rabbi said, "I don't know—but we have to have faith," and blah, blah, blah. After that I never believed in God again. So at that point I was really no longer Jewish, though I stayed at religious school and went through having a bar mitzvah. I did it for my grandfather, a devout Jew who wanted all his grandboys to be bar mitzvahed. He died a month before mine. So the truth is that I didn't feel Jewish in any real sense, which made it all the more galling that I couldn't be in the mainstream of my school. (At that age I so desperately wanted to be accepted, I didn't even question the values of the group I wanted to be accepted by.) Of course, I could never have been in the mainstream anyway—I didn't like country music. So I guess you could say I really was an outsider's outsider. But that frustration may have been the engine of creativity.

As for the *Dead Poets Society* itself, I think it came to me as I noticed that I'd begun using more and more poetry to sort of make my points in the emerging screenplay. It became clear to me that even though the teacher taught English, his focus was going to be on poetry—or at least that's what we were going to see him teach on-screen. So I began building his background as a guy who'd been at the school and a rebel in his own way, and had suffered under the heavy thumb of the school's administration. I thought that if you looked back into his yearbook, there'd be a reference to this sort of mysterious club he'd been a part of, and that that club would have something to do with poetry. The name—the Dead Poets Society—came out of the poets they revered. Disney did not want to release a movie with *Dead Poets Society* as the title. They had ten pages of alternative titles, and the studio's working title was "Keating's Way." Really, nauseating. The production ignored it. To us, it was always *Dead Poets*

Society, even on the slate. The paperwork from the studio used "Keating's Way." It made me very nervous. But finally they embraced it and said okay, but only because they couldn't think of anything better. You know, I think if they'd ever thought to change the name of the club, they'd have solved their problem—but I wasn't going to tell them that.

Of course now, in hindsight, it's easy to say that the movie has the perfect title, and in fact people have told me that the title is what made them want to see the film— the mystery of it, and all that. If I remember correctly, *Honey, I Shrunk the Kids* was called "Itsy Bitsies," or something like that, until *Throw Momma from the Train* came out and did well and that sort of opened the Disney marketing department up to the possibility that titles could be more imaginative. To me, *Honey, I Shrunk the Kids* is a perfect title. You get it right away.

Disney was nervous about *Dead Poets*. Remember, Disney was considered nearly dead in those days, especially before Michael [Eisner] and Jeffrey [Katzenberg] rode in to the rescue. They didn't release many movies back then, and every movie was an event to them—a test of whether they were going to continue to be viable as a company or suddenly find themselves in trouble. *Dead Poets* was unconventional, a Robin Williams comedy in which Robin was not playing a funny guy. He was playing someone who loved poetry and trumpeted it as a way of embracing life more fully, and who wanted his students to feel the same. He wanted to inspire them.

As a kid I was a terrible writer. I was inarticulate and made C's on my writing papers, until I transferred schools in the tenth grade and suddenly started getting A's. Why? Two reasons. One, because I started reading fiction with a passion. Two, I learned the value of revision—the rewrite.

Still, I didn't get interested in writing fiction until college, at Vanderbilt, where I had a fabulous writing teacher named Walter Sullivan. He had a great technique. You'd show up at his class the first day and there'd be seventy-five people enrolled in a class that he said could handle no more than twelve. He'd give a great talk and then announce that by Thursday morning, which was only two days later, everyone who wanted to be in the class needed to slip a ten-thousand-word short story under his office door. Of course he didn't even have to read any of them, because he only got ten or twelve. Those who really wanted to stay in the class wrote the story; those who weren't properly motivated didn't. And then he'd show up on Thursday morning and say, "Well, where is everybody?" It was a brilliant way to weed people out.

The other thing I remember was his telling a story about his own writing teacher, who always told the same story the first day of class and then told the same story again the second day of class as though he'd never told it the first time. The whole class would sit there silently until finally one brave soul would raise his hand and say, "Sir, I hate to tell you this, but you told that story last class." And the teacher would shout, "Of course I did. I was waiting to see if any of you have the courage to speak up. A writer has to have courage!" It was a great demonstration of a great lesson.

So that's when I first became interested, seriously, in

writing. I'd always been interested in movies, so when, in that same semester, in the middle of a novels course, the teacher said that we could, if we wanted, make a super-8 movie rather than do a term paper, most of us did. This was 1969, a time when there was a lot of experimenting. The free university was starting to compete with the pay university, so they were trying to make class as entertaining as they could. I made a little movie based on John Barth's *Lost in the Funhouse* and that was it. I was hooked. I knew what I wanted to do, even though the movie I made was absolutely horrible. To edit it I borrowed a little view box and went down to the art department, where the department head was making movies by simply shooting random footage, cutting the film into two-foot stays and putting them together at random, and turning on music and lights. Everybody went, "Wow, groovy!" As I said, it was 1969.

After graduation I made a short 16-mm film in Nashville and went to work for ImageMaker, a company that produced commercials and industrial films. On weekends I shot one of my shorts, using friends as actors. I realized I didn't have a clue how to communicate to actors. So I enrolled at USC film school in the hope that there was going to be some instruction in that part of the process, but there really wasn't. The only teacher they had to teach directing was a gentleman named Norman Taurog, who by then was in his nineties and blind. I remember his walking in to the directing class with a cane and a guy leading him in and his sitting down and saying, "I suppose you all are wondering how I'm going to critique the performances in your movies when I can't see." And of course that's what we were all thinking. Especially since the movies we were making had no dialogue. And he said, "Well, I can smell a performance by the way the sprockets go through the projector." He wanted us to make only comedies, and he would gauge how good the movies were by how much laughter he heard in the room. I'd ask other instructors about working with actors and they'd say, "Hitchcock didn't know anything about actors—and he did okay." So I left USC after a year and went to study with Jack Garfein, who'd been a film and Broadway director. He had come out to L.A. to open the Actors Studio and the Lee Strasberg Institute, and had then started his own workshop, which was called the Actors' and Directors' Lab.

Occasionally, Jack also brought in his teacher, Harold Clurman, the founder of the Group Theater, a director of many Broadway plays, a prolific writer, the drama critic for *The Nation,* and one of the most impressive and powerful speakers you'd ever want to hear. He'd fly out here every few months and critique the work of the Actors' and Directors' Lab students and then just hold forth—on theater, life, art—and I'm telling you, you'd walk out of his lectures convinced that you could change the world. Of course you'd wake up in the morning and say, "Me? Change the world? Who am I kidding?" But like my fiction professor at Vanderbilt, Clurman was an inspiration for the character of Keating.

Anyway, the whole time I'm studying at the Actors' and Directors' Lab I'm writing, but writing dreck. All kinds of

experimental stuff then, influenced by Antonioni, Bergman, Fellini. And I hadn't yet figured out how to even get
my ideas across. There were only a few moments when I
knew that something I'd written was working. I think you
know when you've found something, because it excites
you, makes you feel like standing up and walking, gets
you physically moving. But it's an odd thing, because
when I was writing *Dead Poets* I was writing speeches
where the teacher would say, "You've got to stand up and
change the world, make your lives extraordinary"—those
sorts of things—but as I was writing that, I was literally
falling asleep.

I usually write a screenplay over a few days—a few days
that follow months, even years, of planning what I'm going to write. And I write so fast because I live in fear
during the writing that my story is going to fall apart. So
when I write I get anxious, terribly anxious.

I don't stop to make sure my punctuation is right, or
that a particular line of dialogue is exactly right; I don't
do any of that until the rewriting process. During the first
draft I concentrate only on, well, finishing the first draft.
It's a kind of all-night, trancelike torture. Knowing what
I'm going to have to go through makes it very much like
going to the dentist; I do anything to avoid it. But once
I'm in the chair, I'll stay there for however long it takes,
because I want to get the pain over with.

Now let me go back for a moment to my gestation and
conceptualization process, the part that precedes the writing. By the time I actually sit down to write I usually have
at least fifty and sometimes a hundred pages of an outline.

It's not a formal outline, though it is scene by scene, with bits of dialogue here and there. The process works a bit like psychoanalysis. I'll make notes and put them in the computer or write them on pieces of paper and throw the paper in a drawer. Then I'll put everything in one computer file, print it out, and then slice apart every paragraph, every line of dialogue, so I have hundreds of separate strips for every idea. I lay it all out on the floor and go around and say, "Here's the beginning," and assemble all the other notes that seem to go with the beginning, then "Here's the next scene," and assemble all the notes that go with the next scene, and so forth. In that way I organize every scene, which is a sort of freeing experience physically because I'm standing up, moving around, looking here and there, and letting other ideas come. It's kind of like building a model on the floor of your room as a kid. When it's all done, I'll take those notes and Scotch tape them down on 8 x 10 pieces of paper and put those pages in a notebook. Then I sit down with the notebook and use it to write the screenplay.

I don't usually write at an office; I use the UCLA law library. I need to be in a place that's phone free, where I can't get on the Internet, etc. I guess you could say I need a prison—a place where there's nothing to do but write. When I had an office I used to go in and straighten up pictures, clean off the streaks on the windows, straighten old paper clips for at least an hour every day before writing. The library is great because I have nothing else to do but start working.

I really don't think there's anything harder than writing.

It's a wonderful torture, but it *is* torture. I'm generally suspicious of anybody who says he or she loves it, because I don't know what there is to love. I think I kind of enjoy that initial free-flowing time of creativity, but then it becomes an incredible discipline. Ninety percent of what you hope will work doesn't work—not in the form you initially imagined it.

I started thinking about *Dead Poets Society* around 1981 and wrote a draft in 1985 that centered on the acting school. When I read it, I gagged and threw it out. The teacher was all right, but the students just didn't work at all. I spent a year thinking that I'd never write the thing, then all of a sudden it hit me what had been wrong and what the setting needed to be, and I sat down and started over.

When I finished, I let my wife read it and then gave it to my agent, who told me, "Gosh, I think this is the best thing you've ever done, but there's no chance of my selling it. If you're really intent on trying to get this done, you better find another agent." So I went looking. The agent I found, I'll never forget going into his office and seeing him with his feet up on his desk. He said, "Well, you know, I've only read half of this but I like what I've read, and I can see this working for some of these young actors coming up." I remember living in fear that the agent would read the second half and then call me up and tell me to get lost. He didn't, but after about six months or so it was clear he wasn't going to be able to sell it. I'd had a couple of meetings on it, and studio executives said the writing sample was really powerful, but wondered what in the world made me think anybody would actually make it. They considered it only a writing sample. One executive who particularly liked it said we should change it into a dance movie, like *Footloose* or *Fame*. He said we could make the protagonist a dance teacher, and we'd rename it the "Sultans of Strut." After that meeting I told my agent I didn't really want to have any more meetings.

A year and a half later, I got a phone call from my agent. He said Steven Haft, the producer who'd read it a year before, had called out of the blue to say he just couldn't get it off his mind and he'd like to take a shot at setting it up. So I had lunch with him and I think he gave me $1,500 for a two-year option on it. He took it in to Roger Birnbaum of Guber-Peters, and then to Jeff Katzenberg at Disney. Katzenberg liked it and bought it. What was ironic was that several of the executives I'd met with on the project had been Disney executives who'd refused to take it to Jeffrey, because they said they were sure he'd never buy it. Jeff told me that they had Robin Williams about to come out in a new movie, *Good Morning, Vietnam,* and they thought he was brilliant in it, so maybe they'd send it to him.

So for two years I couldn't get arrested and now everything was moving quickly. I had been sent low-paying, nonunion things for independent producers. I wrote a script called "Rampage," which was a thriller that got made into a television movie called *Sins of the Father* for ABC. I wrote a seventy-page treatment for a movie called *The Gladiator,* which was sort of a *Road Warrior* set in Los Angeles; it also got made into a movie at ABC. I was hired by A&M Films to do a pretty extensive rewrite on a space opera script I'd written, but it didn't get made. But I was barely eking out a living. I made a short at the Actors' and Directors' Lab that won several awards and almost got me a feature to direct. I cowrote a comedy for a producer who said, "I want you to direct it, but my backers need to see some proof. I'll give you some money and you can shoot one day of the script." A test to see whether I was the right guy to direct it. I shot it, and I thought it turned out pretty well, and then the producer died the day after we finished it. No kidding. He had a heart attack. I hope it wasn't the scene.

By then my tolerance for rejection had, by necessity, grown. I think, in the big picture, that maybe a writer's greatest challenge is having thick skin. Every time you spend six or eight months, or however long it takes you, to conceive of and write a screenplay, and you get very excited about it and you show it to some people and they hate it, or you get a good response but umpteen agents and producers and executives pass, your tolerance for rejection grows, or you quit. In the beginning, when something like that would happen, I'd have to go to bed for literally two or three days. The next time it would take only a day to get over it and then soon I'd lie down for ten minutes and then just sit up and think, "Well, on to the next thing." After several years of this I realized that I had no other professional options. I wasn't trained to do anything else and was too old to go to med school, too old to go to law school, too old to do anything else. I had to make it as a writer.

You end up with this sort of faith in yourself that no

one else can validate. And you end up with a skill and a work ethic. Harold Clurman said that to be a writer you have to go to work every morning, like a grocer. You have to go in at seven o'clock and flip the OPEN sign and start work. You can't gnash your teeth, or sit waiting for inspiration. He was right about that.

I think what's most unusual about *Dead Poets* is that it's a movie about ideas and about the inspiration that ideas can provide. I remember that every time I went to a screening of the film, I had this intense feeling that everyone was going to walk out of the movie at the suicide, because I was afraid it completely undercut the movie's message about the power of ideas and inspiration. When I planned the script and was making my outline, I envisioned some sort of trial at the school for Keating. During the trial, some of his students would have to defend him, to stand up for him. And then it occurred to me that was all they really had to do; literally stand up for him. And I didn't need the trial!

The suicide worried me terribly; it still does. When I go to a movie and the main character dies, I sometimes feel like just getting up and leaving. That death better have meaning. In this case, I hoped Neil's death did.

There was one scene that I particularly liked, which other people tell me they liked, too. It was the scene where Todd, who's shy, is finally able to stand up in front of the class and invent a poem—express himself. Here's this teacher, Mr. Keating, really reaching him, telling him to ignore the laughter of the class, and you can see the boy's struggle and triumph.

Because I'd been thinking about it for five years, *Dead*

Poets Society probably required less rewriting than any script I've done. I think the first draft was about 145 pages, which I cleaned up and got down to 125 pages in the next draft, and that's the draft I sold. One of the main things that changed during production was the idea that Keating was dying of Hodgkin's disease, which I originally decided had motivated his whole carpe diem thing. It got cut, ultimately, because it was kind of a cheat. It's easy for people to rally around—for the students to stand up on their desks for—someone who's dying. People would do that, even if they didn't necessarily believe in what the dying man stood for. With the Hodgkin's disease, it was cheap. Without it, you knew that the boys stood up because they believed in his ideas.

I was very proud of the movie. Peter Weir did a great job and all the actors were wonderful. It never occurred to me that I might win an Oscar—that was just icing on the cake. By then, *Dead Poets* was financially successful, and *Honey, I Shrunk the Kids* was an even bigger success, and I'd gone from a writer struggling to find a job to an Oscar-winning writer in less than a year.

But if I had had any inclination to get a big head, the Oscars cured that. The presenter who gave me my Oscar was Jane Fonda. She had recently been in the news because she had started dating Ted Turner. Anyway, she handed me the Oscar and I made my little speech and we went together into the press room where there was a small stage in front of bleachers filled with about sixty press members, who were supposed to ask the winner questions. Jane and I took the stage and she said, "I'd like to introduce you to Tom Schulman, who's just won an Oscar for best original screenplay. Do you have any questions?" There was a barrage of questions. "Jane, what's it like with Ted? Are you getting married?!," etc. And she said, "Come on, this isn't my night, it's Tom's night. Please direct your questions to him." So there's a little pause and somebody else says, "Tom, what's it like getting an Oscar from Jane? What's your feeling, you think she'll marry Ted?" "That's it," she said, "interview over!" and we walked out. I got the message. I understood where the writer stood in the Hollywood pantheon. So the next day, I went back to work.

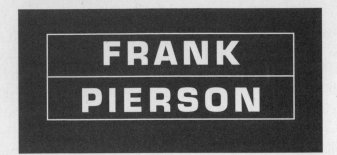

FRANK PIERSON

Frank Pierson is the writer of some of my favorite movies, so I was thrilled when he agreed to speak with me. We met at the deli where he eats breakfast daily with an eclectic and accomplished group of friends. My first question was about *Dog Day Afternoon,* which seems to hold up as well today as it did in 1975.

SOME TIME AGO THERE WAS A DOUBLE-PAGE PHOTO spread in the *Los Angeles Times* of film directors at work. I remember thinking that the directors whose work I found least interesting were the ones whose photos showed them framing the shot with their fingers or pointing at somebody or yelling or what have you. The most interesting directors, like Sydney Pollack, were just sitting and *listening* to what was going on. I think this story bears some relationship to screenwriting, and I'll get to that in a moment. But let me first say that I puzzled over this photo spread for quite a long time, and then finally realized that what it probably has to do with is the nature of theater and performance—that is, the difference between theater and film. Film is projected against a flat screen; it's utterly unreal and fixed in time and space, and nothing can talk back to you; you sit there and have a passive experience. Theater, on the other hand, is an interactive experience, with real actors portraying real emotions—and I think that those directors who were gesticulating so wildly are embarrassed by the emotions they feel in that arena. This is true of many directors, as well as film executives, but it's much less true about writers. And that's how the story is tied in to screenwriting: Writers seem to have a more natural affinity for the stage and for drama—real-life drama. On a film set, if the writer is present, you're not likely to see him watching the action from behind the television monitor; he's probably going to watch the actors, not their images. But these days, directors—especially young directors—tend to watch their scene unfold on the monitor, far from where the actors are performing.

All of which is to say that I think one reason *Dog Day Afternoon* holds up as well as it does—and I think it does—is the performances. They were real performances created by an ensemble of New York actors and directed by a director, Sidney Lumet, who knows how to work with actors. They created a life for the script that still rings true today. What I notice today is that a lot of films, maybe even most, are made on the wave of energy of the moment, riding certain trends and attitudes and feelings that are specific to the time in which they are made, not to anything universal. And to that extent they are going to fade out in time and seem dated.

When I wrote the *Dog Day* script, I included a floor

plan of the set, created from the way I imagined the staging. As it turned out, the only thing that was different was that Sidney twisted it from right to left. My scripts have varying degrees of specificity. Sometimes they're of a film I've already seen in my mind's eye, and sometimes they're less specific. But I tend to do a lot of drafts, which has the effect of making the script more and more specific, because it gets more specific each time. Then I'll let some trusted friends read it, and just the mere fact of knowing that someone is reading it does something to the way I think about the material. Nine times out of ten, I'll hand it to someone and as he's leaving with it I want the script back to begin rewriting again. Suddenly I see it through the other person's eyes. Usually by the time I give it to the producer or director, I'm six or seven drafts in—and that's when the script really begins to open up and take shape as a film. The producer and director read it and see things that I didn't see, or we suddenly realize that I didn't make a particular point clear enough or simply forgot to dramatize something that needed dramatizing.

Dog Day was built not around the failed bank robbery but around the character who tried to pull it off and the other people in his world. I wanted the viewer to continue to learn more about them all the time, like peeling back the onion layers. To do that, the story had to be constructed in a particular way that was a little at odds with the way Warner Bros. marketed the movie as a true story, as reality. Some of the things depicted in the movie happened, and some didn't—I imagined them—but nothing that did happen happened in the movie in the order that it really happened. To be true to the character, though, I had to put these events, real and imagined, in a specific order—an order that kept revealing something new about the main character and also about the way in which the people in the bank lose their fear of him; they begin to identify with him, and in the end they identify with him totally in his battle against the police outside. Then everything turns around when they get to the airport and the police make their move, and then they desert him completely, which is the last thing he realizes—that he's totally alone.

I'll tell you, this movie—the script, really—benefited tremendously from having Sidney direct it, because Sidney likes to have a lot of rehearsal before shooting, almost as though staging a play. He had the actors for about three weeks of rehearsal—and Sidney really knows how to make use of rehearsal time. Most movie directors don't; they don't have the faintest idea how to *really* use rehearsal time. What they usually do is simply use it to work out staging. What Sidney does with it is explore—he uses the actors to help him explore the characters that they're playing. Very often he'll have them improvise, just go off the script, and improvise all the way through. Then they'll come back to the script with the added perspective that these experiments have given them. Well, that was the idea here, that they would rehearse for about ten days or so, and then I'd come back from the other job I was on, see where they were, and do whatever was necessary to incorporate their new insights. As far as I knew at that point, the script was more or less what I'd turned in to him; maybe I'd added a few jokes.

Well, anyway, I'm sitting out here in Hollywood, working, and I get this frantic phone call, "Get on a plane and come to New York!" So I do; I fly there and see everybody sitting around with very long faces. Everything had come to a halt. I said, "What's happened?.," and one of the producers said, "Well, I think that Al was talking about a little dialogue polish here," at which point Pacino just exploded and I said, "Well, it looks to me like Al's not talking about a dialogue polish."

As it turned out, Pacino really wanted to quit the picture. I asked, "What is it, is it the homosexuality? Is that the element of it that bothers you most?" And he said, "No, it doesn't bother me, but I just can't play Sonny the way he is now."

What you have to understand is that this thing had begun with a studio's working title of "Boys in the Bank"— a play on *The Boys in the Band*. And the character played by Chris Sarandon, in real life, was one of those drag queens who can't offer you a glass of water without putting such an obscene sexual spin on it that it makes you fall down laughing. I'd picked up on all of that, and the script was, I thought, hilariously funny. There were a lot more jokes in it, a lot more sexuality, including something that had happened in real life. What happened is that Sonny's "wife," Leon, came to the bank. They actually took him over to the door of the bank to talk. So here were two people who are playing the one scene in their lives that cries out for privacy. They know that their love is doomed, know that they're both doomed, know that everything's going to hell—and they're having to say good-bye with Leon standing on the sidewalk talking to

Sonny, who's standing inside the bank while an FBI man is behind Leon, holding him by the belt so that he can't be pulled into the bank and added to the hostages. We obviously don't know what they really said, so I made up all the dialogue. What we do know, though, is that at the end of the conversation they kissed each other on the lips. That made the crowd, the police, and everybody start screaming and yelling, and one thing led to another. How could you not write that into a screenplay? It's too good.

The theme of the homosexual relationship and what it meant in terms of action, and the things they did were very much in the forefront of the action and the dialogue and everything else. Al said, "I can't do that." And I said, "Well, let's be specific." He said, "The kiss is out, and there can't be any jokes about their relationship. And furthermore, I won't appear in the same frame with Leon." So I said, "In other words, the only way that I can do a scene between the two of you is if you're on the telephone?" And he said, "Yeah." It went on like that for a while longer and the producers said, "What do you want to do?" And I said, "Well, I think it's time to send the script to Dustin Hoffman"—who'd wanted to do it. Pacino said, "Listen, before you do that, I know a little about you, and you've had some ups and downs in relationships. . . ." What he knew is that I'd been divorced. He said, "Let me ask you something: How often in the course of a serious relationship, how often when it comes to the big, big scene where the two people who've discovered they can't go on together anymore and are going to have to say good-bye forever—how often does sex come into it?" And I said, "Never." And he said, "Think about this: Once you establish that a man married a man, you can't take that awareness away from the audience; they're going to carry that in to every scene that they see, and it's going to affect their understanding and feelings about the people as the scene develops. So why couldn't we leave the sex jokes out and do this as a story about two people who love each other and can't find a way to live with each other?" And I immediately said, "Damn! Why in the hell didn't you say that three months ago, when I would've had time to sit down and really work that through? It's brilliant!" And he said, "Well, I wish you'd try now." And I said I would.

So Sidney and I left and went to dinner together. He was deeply upset. I was less so, because I saw this as an opportunity. I thought Pacino was absolutely dead right. Now all I had to do was take the screenplay apart, take everything out, and stitch it back together again. In fact, it turned out to be much easier than I thought it was going to be, and took me only about four hours.

The hardest part was finding a way to do the Leon story through two telephone calls. The answer came partly from reality and partly from my imagination. Here's what I did: I sat down and wrote two long monologues of about four pages each, one for Pacino and one for Sarandon, in which they vomit up absolutely everything that they think about each character, both good and bad. It took about a day to get that worked out. Then I brought it down to the rehearsal set and Sidney dismissed everybody but Al and Chris. I turned on a tape recorder, handed them their sides, and said, "Okay, go." I can't remember now which one of them started, but they began by reading off the paper and then they began improvising, then went back to the paper, and then back to improvising, and so on until it was done—nearly an hour. Then we had about twelve people transcribe that stuff, which is where I took the stuff to use in the two telephone scenes. They were actually cut up and turned into two in order to give both conversations an arc—like a short story that tracks what their real-life relationship was like: It starts out tentatively and then it grows until trust is given, then trust is betrayed, bringing anger and fury, and then there's helplessness, and then there's good-bye, a sad good-bye. It was the odyssey of their whole relationship—and all the while the police are listening, and Leon's not telling Sonny this, which only seems like more of a betrayal.

This illustrates how, in screenwriting, you get to a certain level where everybody is satisfied, but then you begin to explore it further and discover, "Wait a second, there's more here." And it was absolutely brilliant stuff. True, the original script would have been funnier—campier, I guess, more like *Priscilla, Queen of the Desert*—and it would've been entertaining and maybe even as successful commercially. But it would not have had the timelessness that it does now, because it would've been more shallow, and it would probably be considered homophobic. I'm grateful to both Sidney and Al. We had that time to rehearse, which gave Sidney and Al and everybody time to come to grips with what they saw taking form. And because of that, we had the opportunity to fix a weakness in the script—a weakness that would have shown when it was projected forty feet high.

This brings up what is, for me, the hardest thing about screenwriting, and that's organizing the storytelling strategy—the plot. I actually hate plot, as such, and much prefer to let my characters' character determine the action. Yes, dialogue is important; I love making up dialogue, especially insofar as it's used to differentiate the characters and make them each idiosyncratic. What I find helpful, when constructing a character, is to think through a bit of what the character's background is, and in that way let the character begin to tell me, as the writer, what he or she wants to do. Now, in some cases, I've carried on this dossier thing to ridiculous lengths. I remember in *Cool Hand Luke,* when the captain of the prison camp, played by Strother Martin, says, "What we have here, is failure to communicate." The truth is that that line appeared suddenly on the paper in my typewriter, and I looked down at it and said, "That's just brilliant." I loved it, but what I thought was that everybody would attack me for having this undereducated guy, in a prison system in the South, saying something that sounded so, well, educated. So I decided to write a little biography for him; it said he'd worked his way up in the Florida prison system, and if you're going to do that and make it all the way up to captain, you're going to have to pass tests and get past certain barriers—and the way you do that is through education: You must have so many hours of criminology at the state university. I invented his whole life so that no one could question where this guy's sudden erudition came from—but no one ever asked. Still, it kind of informed how I wrote him the rest of the way, so that he began to look like someone who goes to his shack at night and reads a book, and that made him infinitely more interesting and less of a stereotype.

Plot logic has to derive from the characters. The way I work is to think about a character who's gotten into a particular situation, and then decide what he'd say or do to resolve the situation for himself, and then whatever comes out of that drives the next scene—and then I start the process over again to lead to the following scene. I always know what the end of the picture's going to be, but I never know exactly how I'm going to get there. That's the process of discovery that is the most interesting part of writing. Maybe it's because writers are always really writing about themselves, in one way or another.

I grew up in New England and New York, went to Harvard for a year, then volunteered for the infantry during World War II and spent three years in the Pacific, two of them in combat. Most of what I did was lead patrols behind enemy lines, which sounds like a suicide mission but really wasn't, and I'll tell you why. Very soon after I got over there and saw my first bit of action, I ascertained that the average soldier had very little control over his own destiny, because our leaders were clearly not adequate. And I decided that if I was going to get killed, I'd get killed because of my own mistake, not because somebody else fucked up. So I volunteered for this squad that did nothing but go behind enemy lines, and in that way I became a squad leader who could more or less control his own destiny. That was my route to survival.

As it happened, during the war my mother published

her autobiography. It was very patriotic, very sentimental, and became an enormous success. Louise Randall Pierson was her name, and the book was titled *Roughly Speaking*. Well, it was the sort of patriotic, rah-rah thing that the studios were making a lot of during the war, and Warner Bros. wanted to turn it into a movie. But all of the Warner Bros. writers had left to write training films or to serve, so the studio asked my mother if she'd try her hand at writing the screenplay. They brought her out here, to Los Angeles, and put her in a house on the beach in Santa Monica, where she wrote the screenplay that became the movie, starring Rosalind Russell as my mother and Jack Carson as my father. That was the beginning of Mom's good career as a screenwriter for Warner Bros. and RKO.

Anyway, when I came back from the war, I visited her and went to some of those Hollywood parties you hear so much about. At one of them she took me to, I remember seeing Charlton Heston and Orson Welles having this enormous argument. There were about seventy other people in the room, but you couldn't hear anything but these two great voices roaring at each other—and there I am, stuck between them. I'm still deaf from it.

It was clear to me that this business that I was getting a little taste of was something I wanted to be part of some day, but I knew I wasn't yet ready. I was in a very strange state of mind, which looking back on I recognize as some form of what is now called post-traumatic stress disorder. I guess it's not surprising, having been in combat for two years. I went back to Harvard.

Before the war I'd intended to be a biochemist, but now

I wanted to be a cultural anthropologist who studies primitive cultures reacting to the stress created by the modern white man. I had been in New Guinea for a while during the war, near the area where Margaret Mead and Gregory Bateson had gotten famous. Somehow, though, right before I was going to leave to study the Eskimo—how he washed his hair and whether he ate baked Alaska for dessert—I decided that cultural anthropology really wasn't for me after all; and besides, there were no jobs for anthropologists. Which is why I became a correspondent for *Time*. Eventually I moved out here to Beverly Hills, to cover military affairs and movies, and got to sit on the set of every movie that was being made in the 1950s.

A few years later, I decided that I really had to do something else, because I was going to be thirty. So I quit *Time* and started writing for television. I wrote for two years without selling a thing, then shaved my beard and got a job as a story editor for *Have Gun Will Travel,* which was then in its third season. The producer was Sam Rolfe, a terrific guy and the best writing teacher I ever had. Well, a few weeks into the season, Sam got into a fistfight with Richard Boone, the star, and decided he'd had enough. He quit, and since I was the story editor and the only person who knew where all the stories were coming from, I became a producer. After about three years, Boone really wanted to take over the show and I said, "Looks like I'm in your way and I don't want to be in your way, so maybe it's better if I leave." And I did. I went over to Screen Gem as a writer, working down the hall from guys like Carl Reiner, Paul Mazursky, Jack Nicholson, Bob Altman, Bob

Rafelson, and John Cassavetes. All of us got fired the same day, because none of the pilots we wrote were selling. Actually, because of contracts, we really didn't get fired; we got traded across the street, to Columbia, where we were supposed to work on features. Getting fired was the best thing that happened to us. I was asked to do a rewrite on a picture that was in trouble called *Cat Ballou,* and the rest is history, because it turned out to be a surprise hit and it made me a pretty hot writer.

I remember the studio bringing a particular book to me called *Cool Hand Luke,* written by a guy named Donn Pearce. Actually, the whole thing began with Stuart Rosenberg, the director, who'd mostly done television but had a great reputation and really wanted to be a feature director. Well, he'd met a producer, Gordon Carroll, who'd been hired by Jack Lemmon to run Jack's production company, which was really a tax haven kind of thing, but in order to make it legitimate they occasionally had to make some movies without Jack Lemmon in them. So Gordon and Stuart went to lunch in Hollywood at Musso & Frank's Grill, and they talked and decided they liked each other and wanted to do things together and they got a little drunk and walked down Hollywood Boulevard to the old Pickwick bookstore—which is what everybody used to do; they'd go to Musso & Frank's, have a couple of drinks, wander down to Pickwick's, and browse for a while before going back to work at the studio. Anyway, these guys were just looking at the titles and stumbled across a basket of remaindered paperbacks going for, I don't know, nineteen cents or something. I don't know whether it was Stuart or Gordon who pulled this one book out, held it up, and said, "This is a great title"—*Cool Hand Luke*. So they bought the book for nineteen cents, researched to see whether or not the movie rights were available, bought them when they found out they were available—and *then* they read the book. One of them said, "Holy Christ, there's a real movie in there!"

Then they came to me and asked me to write the screenplay based on the experiences this guy Pearce had heard about from other prisoners when he was on a chain gang down South. The original story or legend centered on this enormous prisoner—a black man, by the way—who weighed three hundred pounds and could beat everybody up. The prison guards were terrified of him because if he ever got mad and decided to fight with them, they knew they'd be unable to control him—he was just so big and so strong. And so they set out to break his spirit, even though he hadn't done anything or threatened them. It was just the mere fact of what he was and could be that frightened them, which is the underlying theme of *Cool Hand Luke*; this guy is so cool that he's outside of everything.

During the writing, Stuart and I had a fundamentally different understanding of who the character was. He thought that Cool Hand Luke was an avatar of Christ, which is the reason that all through the movie you see so much symbolism of Luke on the cross, his arms outstretched. Anyway, I kept saying, "No, no, no. This is Camus's existential hero." I considered Luke the man who's set himself apart and cannot be involved. He'll

never do any evil because he's not going to react or respond to anybody in the prison system, which makes him
an absolutely free spirit—which is why the guards attack
him, because they can't bear that. He's the man who es-
capes without even escaping. So we had that discussion
all the time, Stuart and I, and in the end he stuck with
Jesus and I wrote *The Stranger*. It's an odd mix, but the
movie sure works.

Well, in any case, I wrote my first draft, which ran 204
pages, because in order to figure out how this guy happened to get where he was, I had to write for myself what
had happened to him the whole day before he came to
drunkenly cut the heads off those parking meters. I wrote
30 pages, trying to dramatize for myself who he was—
such and such happened and he tried to visit his ex-wife
and the kids and she had some guy there and they got into
a big brouhaha and she threatened to call the cops and he
went and got drunk and then he went to church and
prayed and nothing happened and this and that and the
other thing, and so on and so forth. And then, once I was
clear on it, we took all that junk out and the first scene
in the movie is of him cutting the heads off the parking
meters; it didn't seem so important to dramatize why once
I understood who he was.

Now the script was down to about 135 pages. We sub-
mitted it to Columbia Pictures, which is where Jack Lemmon's company had its deal. They instantly rejected it,
even though Paul Newman was already on board. He'd
committed just on the basis of the book, which in fact is
why Columbia had agreed to put up the money to hire

me to write the screenplay. And now they said no—because they didn't want to do a picture in which Paul died in the end. So we took the script to Warner Bros., and Warner Bros. picked it up immediately and we finished it there. From that point on, all we had to do was just sort of simplify it, to be sure that the story was focused and didn't go off on too many tangents or get into too many details about the subsidiary characters, who were all as interesting as hell but beside the point for the movie; their stories were just there to support Luke's, and to the extent that they didn't, we cut them out.

I did add one rubber-ducky scene. A rubber-ducky scene is a scene where we learn that so-and-so is the way he is because his mother took away his rubber ducky when he was five years old. You see them in movies all the time. In this case, it wasn't that anybody was really asking for a rubber-ducky scene; it's just that I felt that we needed to draw Luke out and dramatize his story more. There's a scene in which the guards come for him and put him in the punishment box for four or five days, with the captain explaining that when a man's mother dies he's apt to get a little rabbit in his blood. It's not supposed to be a punishment, per se; it's that Luke's being put in the box to keep him from running—so it's for his own good. Well, that was going to be a good scene and give real impetus to his deciding to break out of the camp, but I thought it could be made richer by actually seeing his mother. I thought that if the audience had met his mother and knew what kind of character she was and got some sense of what lay behind all this, then Luke's grief, followed by his days and nights in the punishment box, would have a much greater impact. So I wrote that long scene, and invented the kind of woman who'd have Luke as a son. She was, by the way, based on my mother. Except for the Southern drawl, that's how my mother talked, and the way she smoked all the time.

My brother's in there, too, and so am I, in the scene in which Dragline, the character played by George Kennedy, beats up Newman but Newman won't give up. My brother, who was ten years older than me, thought he was doing me a favor and toughening me up by beating the crap out of me all the time. My way of dealing with it was to refuse to give up, so he had to hit me hard enough so that I'd eventually bleed—and if my mother saw that she'd kick the crap out of *him*.

There was also another scene I particularly liked, the one where Luke stops in the rain and everybody gets on the truck and he stands and raises the shovel to the sky and dares God to strike him dead with lightning, but nothing happens and he says, "Just what I thought," and he gets back on the truck. That whole sequence is straight out of existentialist literature. Which is interesting, because somebody once pointed out to me that much of my most successful writing has to do with characters who are alienated from society. I hadn't thought about it before he said that, but now when I look at the Pacino character in *Dog Day* and Newman's character in *Cool Hand Luke* and even, in an odd way, *Cat Ballou,* you do come to that conclusion. I suppose I don't write heroes; I write anti-heroes.

And yet I turned down *Rambo;* I was the first writer they brought it to and I was just so appalled by him—I think because I'm interested primarily in character, and with a character like that, there's no place to go, no room for growth.

One last point. I remember something else about *Dog Day Afternoon* that's probably very instructive about Hollywood. The fact is that Warner Bros. did not want to make the picture at all. The only reason they did was because it was Al Pacino—a hot actor who'd come off of *The Godfather* and had already teamed with Sidney on *Serpico*. They didn't want to make it because they thought the ending was too downbeat.

You hear that all the time in Hollywood: "Why does it have to end like that? Can't it be happier? If he dies in the end, it just turns off the audience." Even when we made *A Star Is Born,* in 1976, we kept hearing, "Does he have to die in the end?" The answer is, "Yeah, if he doesn't die in the end, there's no movie!" I mean, this kind of thing goes way, way back. I actually hauled out and made everybody read the section of the David O. Selznick biography that details the memos sent to him by the studio during the making of the original *A Star Is Born,* in 1936—because they were trying to force *him* to keep the guy alive at the end. Nobody ever learns anything, which I guess is the complement to Bill Goldman's famous line, "Nobody knows anything." You still hear that pictures released in the fall don't make money and that movies in which the hero dies at the end don't make money; stuff like that. Really, nobody learns anything in Hollywood.

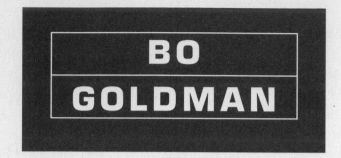

BO GOLDMAN

Spending a few hours with Bo Goldman should someday be the top prize on a game show. He is warm and witty and endlessly entertaining. Everything reminds him of something else, and often the answer to a question is embedded in a breathless story about some character from his past. And oh, what a past he's had. We met for breakfast in a Santa Monica restaurant, and the next time I looked around, the lunch rush had ended.

TALKING ABOUT SCREENWRITING IS VERY DIFFICULT. I feel like an Indian who's having his picture taken. I remember once answering a bunch of questions at a symposium about the little details of how I wrote and what kind of writing instruments I used and all that stuff I'd never really thought about before, and the next day I tried to go back to work and couldn't.

The first person to tell me that I was a writer was the analyst I went to a long time ago. He said, "You are a writer." I didn't really believe him. At the time I still wanted to be Oscar Hammerstein, and had been working for ten years on a musical about the Civil War, and just couldn't get it going. It was really disappointing and knocked all the stuffing out of me, because I'd had a musical on Broadway when I was twenty-six called *First Impressions,* produced by Jule Styne and directed by Abe Burrows. Now I was trying to get the second one on, and it wasn't going well and looked like it never would. I remember my psychiatrist's telling me that Dickens used to think of having a parrot on his shoulder, and every time he got stuck for what to write next, he'd look up at the parrot, and the parrot would tell him what to say. I looked for my parrot for a long time. The kicker to my relationship with this wonderful man came many years later, when *Shoot the Moon* opened the film festival at Lincoln Center. I hadn't seen him in a long time, and he admitted to me that he didn't know much about serious film. I was surprised and asked him, "Have you never seen *Grand Illusion?*" He said, "No, I like the good guys and bad guys."

My father was a very rich and powerful man who began losing all his money in the crash of 1929—three years before I was born. He'd come from the ghetto, one of ten children, and was totally self-made. At one time he owned more than eighty retail stores, most of them in steel towns around Pennsylvania like Hazleton and Wilkes-Barre; and upstate New York around Elmira and Binghamton and Utica and Syracuse; and East Chicago, Indiana, and Moline, Illinois—all these places. To me, it was as though I'd been born a child of a vaudevillian who'd played the Palace. And then I saw Wilkes-Barre and I saw the piles of coal around the mouth of the mine, and all the soot. When I was born, my father was forty-two but looked sixty, though he had the energy of someone who was twenty. Evidently, it was a kind of style: Young Jews from the ghetto tried to look older than they really were. When he was fourteen, he was supporting his family, and later several of his brothers and sisters ended up embezzling from him. Anyway, he had a lot of interests and was a real character, completely charming and charismatic. He was the founder of the Goldman Trophy, which is the Davis Cup of bridge—the eastern pairs championship—the oldest and most valued trophy. He was also FDR's intimate. Roosevelt had been his attorney, after he was assistant secretary of the navy.

Father also dabbled in the theater. He loved it. In those days the term for it was "late money." If you were out of town with a show and having some problems and wanted to stay another couple of weeks to work things out before you got to New York but all the capital was used up, you went to a late-money guy. Father did a little of that, because nothing excited him like the theater. He took me to see shows as often as he could. It didn't matter how hot a ticket was, he'd call the Supreme Ticket Office—Big and Little Willie Deutsch—and say, "Big Willie, I need top seats," and he'd get them. I don't know how, because we were really more middle class then, not colossally wealthy the way Father had been before the Depression. Our life was like a sepia print of the past. We were living in a big, old, rent-controlled apartment on Park Avenue that was right out of *Sunset Boulevard,* with all the rococo furnishings. But then there'd be echoes of glory, like theater tickets. I suppose that was the only real past glory Father could recapture; he couldn't go deep-sea fishing in the Sea of Cortez anymore, or travel the world on ocean liners, or have a racing stable in Chantilly, France; he could only go to the theater. Every few months my mother would say, "Which Ming vase should we break now?"—for the insurance. It was quite Gothic. I ate a lot of rye bread before dinner was served and got very fat—and really have never been able to lose it all. Father would blow up at the table. Seeing *Long Day's Journey into Night* made me cry, because Father was very similar to O'Neill's father, the James Tyrone character. He'd come into the room and take over. I remember an early session with my shrink, telling him that I thought I was just the average son of a tyrannical Jewish ex-tycoon, and he said, "Everybody's unique," which is of course the first thing you have to learn in order to be a writer. Father asked me once what I wanted to be, and I said a playwright, and he said, "You haven't suffered enough." I guess he didn't realize his effect on me.

I think the one way I was really like my father was that I couldn't get enough of the theater. I think that was partly because I could see him there and see him happy—or happier. We went to see *Bloomer Girl,* a wonderful musical by Harold Arlen and Yip Harburg—in fact, Father went to see it twice, something he did rarely. He said, "I want you to see this. I think you'll like this, Bobby," which was my name then. Before we went in he said, "There's a chorus boy, second row, with big teeth—marvelous," and when the same performer's big number was on, I think it was "I Got a Song," Father pointed at him and said, "There he is, there he is. That's good. That's good." He just loved it. Here's this guy who'd been a big shot once, and this was all he had—except for finding a way to send his children to the best schools. Exeter and Princeton. My two older brothers went to Exeter, but I failed the exam, and knew I would; I was terrified and froze up and had to go to summer school before getting in. My first year there I came home for Thanksgiving, but my brother Douglas went to Nashua, New Hampshire, to a friend's home. What happened to him on that trip and in its aftermath became the basis for the story for *Scent of a Woman.*

It began on Wednesday afternoon, the day before Thanksgiving. He and his friend went to the Boston Bruins game that afternoon, and his friend brought a pint of cheap whiskey. Douglas never drank, but they drank the whole thing on the train from Boston to Nashua. So what happened was, my family and I are all sitting down for Thanksgiving supper in New York, and my father's bemoaning the fact that Douglas didn't come home for Thanksgiving—he considered it an act of rebellion. Then the phone rings. It's five to one in the afternoon, and it's the dean of Exeter saying that Douglas had been hopelessly intoxicated on the train and that his friend's father had called him to say he was worried, and they were bringing him back to the school infirmary. Next thing you know my father's on a train to Exeter, calling on all the members of the committee who are going to expel him for intoxication—for embarrassing the academy in public. He knocked on all the doors and said, "I was betrayed by another father. I grant you my son shouldn't have done this . . ." That's where the line in the script came from, because he'd signed an agreement that granted in loco parentis control. The agreement said that whoever was inviting the student would be in charge and have full parental authority. Well, Father's pleas didn't fall on deaf ears. I heard later that it was a very vigorous fight in the faculty meeting. In the meantime, Douglas had to go for six months to a little cheesy school that took in kids who'd been kicked out of the more prestigious schools. I asked him what it was like and he said, "What can I tell you, F.B.?"—F.B. was short for Fat Boy.

So here's how that morphed into *Scent of a Woman*. In about 1990 I get a call—my oldest brother, Chester, was in the drunk tank at Lenox Hill Hospital. Chester was this kind of Gatsby-like character, a self-made guy, immensely successful, always trying to pass in Gentile society. And now he was an alcoholic. I came back to California very depressed, I didn't have work, and I heard about this project that Martin Brest had been trying to do for years, a remake of the Italian film *Profumo di Donna*, about an army cadet who goes along with a blind army officer on a trip. So I went over to Universal to watch this movie in a screening room, and I was in no mood to like it. The minute I saw Vittorio Gassman, I realized that this was Chester. And then I noticed that the character was wearing the same clothes as Father. I said, "I'll do it," because I understood everything about

the story. It was really a merging of Chester's story—
a guy with a past who has a drinking problem but is
still charming and charismatic and unpredictable—and
Father's story. The second element was the kind of betrayal of my brother Douglas at Exeter; sure, it's bent
and turned, because the real issue is whether the kid will
inform, as opposed to my friend's father, who did. The
third element that contributed had to do with my two-
year stint in the army, where I had a first sergeant in
basic training, a Nisei from the 442nd Regimental Combat Team, which was the most highly decorated unit in
the army. He was the most terrifying person I've ever
known—and yet the one I respected the most. He called
me in once and told me I'd done a good job, and that
meant something to me. So I think the character of Slade
(played by Al Pacino) had some of his resonance. There
was something of the night about both of them. Now,
obviously, some of those influences on me when I was
writing were subliminal, not conscious. It's only years
later, when you look back, that you see them and can
say, "Oh, yeah, that's because . . ."

My first real taste of writing had come at Exeter, where
I ran the school newspaper. I got the job when the kid
who had been the managing editor got kicked out for
drinking. That came in handy when Chester bought a re-
gional newspaper upstate. He did it to save the family,
because he'd figured out that there was money to be made
in weekly newspapers, which have to sell space for legal
notices. His idea was to buy the Democratic weekly up
there and get all the advertising—and that way we'd be

in the black. He persuaded my mother's brother, who owned liquor stores and a real estate business and an insurance company in the Bronx—a man I think secretly paid our rent on Park Avenue—to loan him the money.

My uncle was another character. He was like a button man in the Mafia: very quiet. Sunday afternoon at five was when he'd wake up, then he'd come visit his little sister, my mother, in Manhattan. She'd fix him, religiously, scrambled eggs. They loved each other. Anyway, I began to write the paper's household hints column, pretending to be five different housewives. I was eighteen. The paper's editor was a really famous guy named Stanley Woodward. He'd been the sports editor of the *Herald Tribune,* and had actually coined the term "Ivy League" to apply to the eight colleges; he also found Red Smith. One day he assigned me the lead article about the trial, which was dragging on and on, of some airman at an upstate base who'd held up a gas station. Well, I wrote this story off of previous stuff, and on the day the paper came out, the telephone rang. It was the boy's mother. She said, "You Jews. Can't you let go of it? Don't you have anything else to put in?" I apologized, because I thought she was right. Not Stanley, though. He was listening to the conversation and took his huge Underwood typewriter and threw it at me. He said, "Don't you ever again apologize for anything you write."

That stuck in my mind, and I connected it to something later, when I overheard Stanley talking to my father, telling him why ours was a lousy newspaper. That really impressed me, for some reason. I knew he didn't have to work there—he'd been retired, after all—and didn't have to drive a hundred miles to put up with all the aggravation. But for him this wasn't just some job; it was about a sense of dedication. He cared more about what the product was, and was trying to show that if the product was good, the people would come. That had a big effect on me.

The thing I've striven the most for in my life is to produce art. I'm an artist. Screenwriting just happens to be the way I express it. I try to protect and enhance the profession. I remember the first Writers Guild Awards presentation I went to, for *One Flew Over the Cuckoo's Nest*. I didn't know anything from awards and didn't want to go, but I went anyway. I was shocked at the contempt I saw—the putting down of producers and studios. I wondered why these people were so angry, so disrespectful to themselves. I didn't know because I hadn't really been around Hollywood long; *Cuckoo's Nest* was my first film. It took me a while to see how writers were held in contempt.

Sometimes someone'll ask me what I do, and I say I'm a screenwriter, and he'll say, "Yeah, I know, but what do you write? The words?" I say, "Yeah, I do that." Then he'll say, "What about what comes next?" So I say, "Yeah, that too." A lot of people don't understand the process, and have contempt for what they can't see being done.

I remember when I was just struggling, starving as a writer, and I was brought in to produce this show at CBS called *Calendar,* which was a kind of magazine show like

Dateline. We were given an hour of prime time at 10:00 P.M. in the summer, when the summer was nothing in television. We had no money, no budget. Andy Rooney and I cowrote everything. He and I had met when we were both working on *The Morning Show with Will Rogers Jr.,* a competitor of *Today;* I was writing ins and outs, and he was my head writer. One of the hosts of *Calendar* was the newsman Harry Reasoner; the other was an actress named Mary Fickett, who'd played Eleanor Roosevelt on Broadway in *Sunrise at Campobello.* Well, we'd do these dumb things about nothing, like how to prepare a show like this. So one of the pieces was supposed to be a day in the life of Mary Fickett, and Andy said we should get one of the news photographers to follow Mary from the time she got up in the morning. He said, "You do it," and I said, "I don't know how to do this. That's what directors are for." He said, "You do it." So I got the cameraman and found little things along the way, like this hundred-foot pole in front of Cartier that they use to clean those huge windows, and a guy preparing pretzels. I was looking for whatever those usually unnoticed things and moments were that made up life on the street as Mary walked by in the early morning. Well, Andy saw the footage that he was going to write the script to, and he told me, "Bo, you know what a thing is." *You know what a thing is.* Those were the words, and I've been using them ever since to describe what I think my talent is—it's knowing what a thing is, knowing what the dramatic possibilities for a thing are and recognizing what it means to life. I approach writing the way Michelangelo approached a big block of marble or granite from which a statue was trying to fight its way out. The pain that you go through to free a story is incredible. I do enormous amounts of research, and I don't have a computer; I finally stop researching when I can't stand it anymore—and then I go write the movie.

I got the assignment for *Cuckoo's Nest* at a time when I was basically homeless, living at a friend's decrepit house in Brewster, New York, with my wife and our children; there was no furniture, just cots. I mean, for years I'd been a writer for TV variety shows, including the Emmys, the Ice Capades, and Andy Williams, but now I'd really bottomed out in terms of work. I was lucky to have a small regular gig at PBS. My big assignment at the time was writing and producing a Christmas show called *An American Christmas in Words and Music*. The director was Ed Sherin, who'd directed *The Great White Hope* on Broadway; in fact, James Earl Jones, who'd starred in the play, was one of our guests.

As it happened, Ed's movie the year before, called *Valdez Is Coming*, based on an Elmore Leonard book, had really flopped, but the star of the movie was Burt Lancaster. So when we were talking about who could host the show, Ed suggested Burt. I thought he was crazy. But I called Universal, where Burt had his offices, and he said to send him the script, and when he read the script he said yes. "But Bo," he said, "do me a favor and spell my name with a 'u' instead an of 'e.' " Wonderful guy. Anyway, we got terrific notices, and Ed and I got to talking about work and the like, and I sort of commented on how my old friends, the guys I'd grown up with, had real jobs and careers, like being partners in law firms, or the head of pediatrics at a hospital. Me, I was nothing and had six children I couldn't support. I was forty and miserable and the thought crossed my mind that sometimes, when you can't put food on the table or pay your rent, you want to kill yourself. Ed said, "You ought to make a movie of that." He encouraged me to put my life on paper. And that became the script, at least an early version, of *Shoot the Moon*, which is really about the contract of trust that a husband violates with his family.

Well, Ed gave the script to his agent, who was the wife of the guy who'd shot some of the stuff for the Christmas show. She didn't like it. Then a guy named Stuart Millar, who'd produced *Little Big Man*, which was directed by Arthur Penn, who'd been the next to last director on my musical about the Civil War that was never mounted, the one I'd worked on for ten years that had put me in the position of being forty and broke and useless—Stuart read it and started shopping it around and Peter Bart ended up reading it. He was head of Paramount then. In time the script became kind of famous in Hollywood for being one of the best scripts that wasn't made; there are really lists like that in Hollywood, of great scripts that aren't made. Peter called me to come out to Hollywood to meet with him and Arthur Hiller, who was going to direct *Starting Over*, because they'd seen the script of *Shoot the Moon*, and they thought maybe I could adapt the book. We met on a weekend, and they said I had the job, so I left PBS and we—my wife and kids and I—came out and lived on Pacific Coast Highway in one of those one-room places. Then I got fired from *Starting Over*. But right before I was going to go back East, I got a little job from Harold Hecht, who'd produced *Marty* and *The Sweet Smell of Success*. He was now an old man and wanted to do a sequel to *Cat Ballou*, which he'd also produced. So I sat down to do a treatment that was really kind of eloquent; it would've made a good short story for a Western quarterly. Harold read it and said to me, "This is really beautifully written. But sometimes what we do is, we just have a page, one page, and we just put a couple of ideas on the page—then we have room for more. And we make another page." He didn't want to work his way through to find out what the movie was about; he just wanted a few words.

I thought then that I'd better go home for sure, back to New York. In fact, my wife did leave, to go back to reopen her fish store. Then I got a call from my agent. He said that Milos Forman had read the script for *Shoot the Moon* and liked it and wanted to talk to me about *Cuckoo's Nest*. I'd read the book, years before, but had never seen the play. When I read the draft of the script they sent over, I fell asleep; I really did, I fell asleep. Milos said, "So what do you have in mind for me?" The first thing I said was, "When McMurphy arrives at the institution, let him laugh and kiss one of the guards." He said—and you have to say this with his Czech accent— "That's good. That's good." What he told me was that he'd talked to twenty writers, and every one of them had a theory about how to adapt the script—but I was the first person to say something concrete, something that could actually be in the movie and wasn't philosophical. I guess it was "that thing"—knowing what "a thing" is, to use Andy Rooney's phrase. Besides, I felt like I was McMurphy. Just as I later on felt like Melvin Dummar, from *Melvin and Howard*. I knew those guys, I identified with them, because I was them. In fact, I remember a pretty big agent once telling me, "You're always writing the same story, over and over." And he was right; I do. I never forget anything. I'm haunted, in a way, by everything that's happened to me and everything I've seen. The past is present for me, and it always comes out in the writing, so the same story gets told in a lot of different ways.

I'd go to the hotel where Milos was staying, to have script meetings. It would be ten in the morning, and he'd be having black bread and cabbage and Czech beer. The room was L-shaped, and I remember one day he took the script and disappeared around the corner for a minute, and when he came back, he was McMurphy. And I thought, "This is good. This is good." Like my father pointing at the Broadway stage—"This is good." I forgot I was the writer; I was just sitting there at the table listening to him.

Milos gave me what's probably the best and most useful note about screenwriting I've ever gotten. I'd come in with pages and he'd say, "Bo, it must be real. This is outside life." What that means is that you can have funny and quirky and strange and screwball, but it's got to be *inside*

life and take place within the boundaries of human experience. If it doesn't, there's no life at all in the script,
and there'll be no life to the movie. "Inside life" is just
other words for Andy Rooney's comment about knowing
"what a thing is." None of that comes easily. You've got
to search for it.

MARC NORMAN

I remember passing a friend of mine in the theater lobby after seeing *Shakespeare in Love*. "I envy you," I said. "I wish I could see it again for the first time." This is a wonderful film, and the story of how it finally got to the screen after an odyssey of many years was told frequently when it came out. What annoyed me at the time, even before I met Marc Norman, was how little credit he got for the film's success. We sat in his office on the grounds of his beautiful home in a coastal canyon. I began by asking him to reflect on his "overnight success"—thirty years in the making.

I'VE ALWAYS SEEN WRITING AS THE MAKING OF something—just the way that I made model airplanes when I was a kid, or the way that I made furniture when I was in my thirties. It's about creativity. Over the years I've found that the one thing I'm most interested in is creativity, in all its forms. I'm mystified by it. Very few people perceived *Shakespeare in Love* as a movie about creativity, but that's how it began.

Starting off, I realized that, if nothing else, I had this

great brand name. Shakespeare's like Mickey Mouse: Everybody in the world knows him. But unlike Mickey, Shakespeare's not universally beloved. So I thought if I could take this brand name and turn it into something charming and entertaining, I'd have something.

Before Tom Stoppard got involved, the script didn't have any inside, English-major jokes. I decided early on that I wouldn't do that. There would be lots of humor—black humor, parodying show business—because I felt that was perfectly valid to that world. But I didn't want to have any erudite esoteric references that might be awkward for somebody in the audience who didn't know, for example, who John Webster was that would take them out of the movie. I didn't want anybody to have to know anything at all about Shakespeare in order to enjoy the movie, outside of the fact that he was a playwright whom they'd probably had to study once or twice in high school, under duress. I wanted that audience included. And in order to include them I had to set up certain rules. My job was to make it so you didn't have to have any prior knowledge of Shakespeare. I wanted to reveal Shakespeare as the movie went on—to tell you everything you needed to know about him as it happened, just the way you do with any other character. While I was writing, I imagined a sixteen-year-old inner-city kid watching the movie; I'd constantly turn to him in my mind and say, "Are you getting it? Are you intrigued? Are you enthralled? Are you with this movie?" And if he said no, I'd stop and rethink what I was doing.

In some ways my model was *Amadeus*—you didn't

have to know anything about Mozart to love that movie. In fact, some people have told me that they learned to appreciate Shakespeare from my movie the way they'd learned to appreciate Mozart from *Amadeus*.

As it turned out, the movie did have some inside jokes. Tom Stoppard put them in, and I actually think they work—the way they were done. I'm very grateful to Tom for what he wrote, just as I believe he's grateful to me for what I wrote. It really took the two of us to get the picture made.

There are two ways to make a living as a screenwriter. The first is by selling spec scripts—doing only what interests you. The other way is by hiring yourself out on assignment. Guys writing only on spec, God bless them. It's a ballsy way to go. They figure they'll write what they want to write, maybe they'll sell it and maybe they won't. If they don't, then they go on to the next thing. I admire that, but I don't know how you raise a family that way. Myself, I have all sorts of internal trepidation. I'll tell you some words of wisdom someone told me a long time ago. He said that you can make a fortune writing in the movie business, but you can't make a living. Sure, someone may buy this script from you for a ton of money, but doing it over and over for a lifetime is hard.

The way to have a real career as a writer is to hire yourself out. That's not to say that you can't do both; I certainly have. But when you do hire yourself out, the thing you have to remember is that you better put some passion on the page. These guys who hire you are renting your passion. If you yourself aren't passionate about the project, you're not going to do a very good job. Let's say the story is about someone stealing some diamonds. Then you have to find something about stealing diamonds that excites you. So what you do is, after wasting a certain number of days thinking about how to get passionate about diamonds, you think, "Well maybe I won't get passionate about the diamonds; maybe I'll get passionate about why the guy needs the money, or maybe I'll get passionate about why the guy is turning back to crime when he wasn't going to do it anymore." Something like that. That's how you find a way to bring some kind of personal agenda to the assignment.

I grew up in L.A., in a world that had absolutely nothing to do with Hollywood. Everybody from other parts of the country assumes that if you live here, your uncle works at the studio. Not true. In my case, my uncle didn't even run the dry cleaners that did Paramount's costumes. I had no contacts. Zero. The one thing I did have, growing up in Los Angeles, was the experience of seeing movies being made. Sometimes they would make them on my street. I'd be driving with my mom through Hollywood and pass a movie studio lot and see behind the wall—the tops of the scenery, crenellated castle tops. It turned me on.

Anyway, I was taking my master's in English at Berkeley with every intention of being a college professor—not so much because I wanted to teach English but because I didn't know at all what I wanted to be, and being a professor was probably as good as anything. But as time went on, I started to dislike it more and more. I'd been a good student as an undergraduate, but when I got into the master's program I began to kind of abhor what I was doing.

As an undergrad, you could kind of pick and choose the stuff you liked to read, aside from the obligatory stuff. As a grad student, you had to like everything and know about everything. That was the mandate of my master's orals— know everything from *Beowulf* to LeRoi Jones. The more I started to dislike school, the more I started to go see movies, as a way of avoiding studying. I remember this little revival theater in Berkeley. You'd go in there and sit on folding metal chairs and see these 16-mm prints of *Nosferatu* and *Red River* and *Citizen Kane,* things like that, all the great movies. And as you'd leave you'd see this sign-up sheet, and you'd get this mailer with a one-paragraph blurb about the upcoming movies. It was written so well—each blurb made me dying to see that movie; the prose in the paragraph was so evocative. There wasn't a movie I didn't want to see; I wanted to see them all. Well, who was writing the paragraphs? Pauline Kael. Pauline Kael was running that theater in Berkeley. She was an Oakland housewife, the bored wife of a lawyer. She'd always loved movies and ended up buying this theater to show her favorites.

Anyway, I guess from that and other things, I had an idea of what a good movie was. I guess I just didn't think I had it in me to work in that world, which is why I kept studying for my master's orals. I took them and just froze; I choked; I kind of blundered my way through. At the end of the orals the three professors on the panel said, "Well, Mr. Norman, we're going to pass you. But we don't recommend that you pursue a further career in education."

To tell you the truth, I was kind of relieved, even though I didn't have a Plan B. And then I thought, "Gee, I like seeing all these movies. Maybe I'll go down to L.A. and see if I can get in the movie business." What a left-field idea. This was 1964. The movie business was the hand-maid of consumerism for any sixties college student. It was like making napalm. That gave me a certain arrogance. I thought, "I'll show up there with my master's degree and my Phi Beta Kappa pin, and they'll think I'm the Second Coming. They'll meet me at the train." And so I came down here and I couldn't get arrested. My philosophy at the time was that I was going to be a failure at whatever I ever did; it just seemed to be in the cards. All I knew about Hollywood was the real superficial stuff I'd read, Benchley and Fitzgerald tottering drunk around the pool at the Garden of Allah. What I took from that was that you could be kind of an alcoholic failure in Hollywood and still meet girls and have a good time. Hollywood didn't seem like a bad place to fail, not like failing, say, in Detroit.

I didn't know what I wanted to do. I just knew I wanted to be on a movie set. For a while I thought about being a script supervisor and then going into directing, because you got to be on the set. I thought that's where people were having fun. I had that whole outsider's dream image thing, that those people are all in there laughing and screaming and screwing around and having a good time making movies.

In my mind the studio was a wall, and I just had to get over the wall; then I would worry about what to do next.

I'll tell you how green I was—I'd go to studio personnel offices and fill out job applications. There'd be a box on top that asked what position I was applying for. I'd put down *producer*. The personnel guy would say, hiding his smile, "Well, we don't have any openings for producer right now, but we've got you on file and we'll call you if anything turns up." I don't know why, but Universal called me back one day. They said they'd looked over my application and were impressed by my education and asked if I'd be interested in taking a job in their executive training program. And I said yeah, that might work— "What would I be doing?" And they said, "Delivering the mail." And I said no, no way, not me.

That night I went to a bar in West Hollywood. Turned out to be a bar filled with wannabe Hollywood guys. I got to talking to two of them and told them what had happened that day, that I'd been offered a job delivering mail, and they said, "You didn't take it?!" They were incredulous. One guy said, "Schmuck. That's the best offer you're ever going to get in your life." So the next day I called Universal back and took the job. The guy was right. The job paid sixty-five dollars a week, and I got ordered around by every temp secretary on the lot. But there was one really good thing about it: The unspoken tradition in the mail room was that you could hustle without fear of getting in trouble; you would not be punished or fired for sticking your head into somebody's office and saying, "Can I come in and talk to you? I want to be in the movie business. Can I wash your car?" That was the unspoken perk of the job—the only perk of the job. Took me six months to get out. It was like my orals all over again.

The way I got out, I went to a producer on the lot named Roy Huggins, who'd done *The Fugitive* and was starting a series called *Run for Your Life*. At that point I was trying to get a job as a production assistant, and I told him I wanted to be a PA. He said, "I don't need a PA. I need writers, I need stories, I'm starting a series. Can you write?" He said he'd buy a story from me as fast as anybody else, and told me about the premise of the show, which was that this guy has a fatal illness and is trying to pack forty years of living into one. So that night I went home and wrote a couple of stories, ten pages each, and I brought them in to him the next day. He read them both and said, "Not this one, but I'll buy this one." That was my first credit, in 1965.

So Universal executives, in their wisdom, noticed that they had a guy who could write, so they made me a casting director. I did that for six weeks and hated it. Then I went off the lot and began working for a producer, Leonard Stern, who was starting a new series called *Get Smart*. I didn't work on the series; I worked for Leonard. He was looking to make other TV pilots and would come up with ideas. He'd tell me the idea for the pilot and I'd write a network presentation for it, ten to twenty pages that fleshed out the idea and made it into something he might sell. And that was fine, except there was a little worm inside me saying, "Gee, maybe you should market yourself as a writer, instead of using writing to get somewhere else." That job went on for about a year and a half, writing every day—then I got kind of tired of it, and when I went in to tell Leonard it was time for me to move on, he suggested that I go to New York and work for David Susskind and Dan Melnick, his partners. So I did. I was there for six months, but I'd met my wife-to-be by then and I was getting homesick. I wanted to come back to Los Angeles and write a screenplay. It was a hot summer. I sat in the kitchen of my little apartment in West Hollywood, sweating in my underpants, and tried to write a screenplay. And when it was done I got an agent who couldn't sell it but he did get me other jobs with it, using it as a writing sample. That's how I started, doing little jobs, like rewriting a TV episode.

For the first ten years of my writing career, the stuff I wanted to write was the stuff I'd watched on TV as a kid, Westerns and adventure movies. I thought I would be happy to be one of the grunts, a proletarian screenwriter. It really wasn't until I got into writing that writing kind of snuck up on me.

The first feature job I got was writing a movie called *Short Ends.* A producer at Columbia named David Swift had had some success with a movie called *The Interns,* and he wanted to do the same sort of thing, this time with young film students instead of young doctors. When he hired me, I pointed out to him that I'd never been a film student and he said shut up about that. So I did.

That project was the worst working experience I ever had. Swift partnered me with a young woman who had actually been a film student. We were kind of Hollywood starstruck kids, and they gave us offices on the lot and we got to drive on every day and park and walk in, and film stars were all around us—this was when Columbia was still an active studio. We were as happy as pigs in shit. But every week Swift would ask to see pages; he'd usually ask to see them Thursday night, and we'd have to hand in what we'd done. And on Friday, he'd say things like, "You two are the worst writers I have ever seen. You have no talent. What makes you think that you can write? How dare you take this money?" Total soul annihilation.

Well, we finished the script in about six weeks and handed it in. Swift then handed it to his bosses, who handed it back; their comment was, "Who wants to see a movie about film students?" Within minutes, the other writer and I packed up our boxes and were gone. Every day for a while, we'd call each other up and talk, like two people who'd been through some terrible disaster together and could only share it with each other.

Now I look back on that job fondly, because nothing since has been as bad. It did something else for me. It made me realize that I kind of liked sitting in a pool of my own sweat. Writing had begun to sneak up on me. I remember a friend of mine saying to me early on that you better love the process of writing, because in the end that's all you're ever going to have. The praise and the blame you can't control. All you can really expect from the work is the satisfaction you get from doing it. That made a lot of sense, and as time went on I saw how true it was.

Naturally, I piss and moan when I'm doing it, but

there's nothing like the excitement of taking on something new and not knowing where it's going, and giving it everything you can find it in yourself to give, and crossing your fingers, and hoping that it turns out right. I don't want to romanticize it too much, but writing is essentially the behavior of an addict; it's kind of an addict's appreciation of a thing.

I suppose every writer has a different standard for knowing when the writing's going well. For me, it's when I surprise myself. Sometimes I can get into this zone where stuff just comes, as though someone's whispering in my ear. When the work is going well, I'm not aware of the day passing, and I wake up in the morning having dreamed scenes. Look, I don't know how to get into the zone; I just know that if I keep pounding my head long enough, it seems to happen.

I remember hearing Anthony Minghella say that writers are directors who, for some reason, choose not to direct. What I took that to mean is that writers see the movie in their mind, they cast it, design the sets, pull the costumes—they do everything. No, it may not match the movie that comes out in theaters, but it is a version—a distinctly valid version—of the movie.

One thing I often do when I write is cast known actors in my mind. Now, they may get fired or hired as the script progresses, but I find it's helpful to imagine real, flesh and blood, skillful actors playing the roles. Ten years ago, when I first thought of Viola in *Shakespeare,* I think I put Meryl Streep in the part; and I think Tom Hanks was Will. When I wrote *Oklahoma Crude* in the early 1970s, I remember putting Audrey Hepburn and Humphrey Bogart in the lead roles, which later turned out to be George C. Scott and Faye Dunaway. I need those stand-ins, because I usually don't have detailed character sketches before I start work. My characters tend to evolve in the course of writing and rewriting, which is why my stand-ins get fired and hired.

I'll tell you one thing I've noticed, and it's absolutely true for me. My best writing has been on the scripts I wrote as suicide notes to the industry—sort of, "Fuck you, guys, I'm outta here. This is the last script you'll ever get from me. I'm tired of this. I'm going to put everything I know into this one and if you don't buy it, 'See ya!' " I've reached that point, I'd say, five, six, maybe seven times; I've been so frustrated and pissed off, so self-blaming, so disgusted with what I've gotten myself into and the shame of what I had to do for a buck, that I said, "I'm getting out of the business after this one last piece of writing, something that expresses me, what I want." One of those scripts, by the way, was *Shakespeare in Love*.

I don't remember too much about working on *The Killer Elite*. One thing I do remember is meeting Sam Peckinpah (the director) for the first time. You have to realize that Peckinpah was kind of considered a force of nature at the time. His secretary showed me into his office the first time I met him. In the office was a foldout couch, and lying there in crumpled sheets was Peckinpah— naked and scrawny. And the secretary said, "He'll be ready in a minute," and she gave him a big vitamin B_{12} shot in the ass with this huge syringe. And then he got up and sort of scratched his nuts, put on some clothes, and said, "Let's get to work." And I thought, "Wow, this is the big time."

Now, at that point, I considered myself kind of a neophyte; I'd been in the business only about ten years and was still pretty green. Peckinpah knew it—he had me for lunch. That's what he wanted to do with the script anyway—chew it up and spit it out, just shoot the movie on the fly.

Now, if you ask why everyone always wants to have the screenwriter for lunch and then chew up and spit out his screenplay, there's a pretty good answer, I think, in the movie *Almost Famous*. It comes when the kid calls Lester Bangs and Bangs says something like, "Hey, you think you're cool. You're not cool. You're a writer. Writers are never cool." And of course he's right. Writers are never cool. Writers are just delicious game for anybody.

Another reason, I think, is that the writer is the one person on the picture who does what he does alone. Everything else about movie-making is a social experience, so everyone else has to interact with people; and you can observe what they do—you know what they get paid. But the writer goes out and does what he does alone. So when he's interacting, it's usually either to tell people what he's going to do, or he's hearing from people about what's wrong with his ideas—and then he goes off alone again to fix them. Studio executives don't know what the writer's going to go do. Is he writing it in an hour? Is he writing it in six months? Does he get someone else to do it? They don't know. They don't know what's happening. The whole thing is the loner going into his cave and evoking spirits.

Does winning an Oscar change anything? Not too much. Here's an example: There's a guy I met thirty years ago, a science-fiction writer. We began a correspondence a long time ago that has moved into e-mailing. Well, he recently wrote to ask me about my USS *Indianapolis* project, which I'll tell you about in a minute. He wrote, "When it goes, you could do me a favor"—get him a job on the film. And I said, "Yeah, when and *if* it goes; I don't know if it's going to get made." And he wrote back, "Gee, I thought you were a made man." And I wrote back, "Nobody in this town is a made man, the highest you can get is hit man."

Well, the truth is that there are some made men. Steven Spielberg is certainly made. And I think there are even some made writers, like Robert Towne and Paul Attanasio and Steven Zaillian. I'm not. I'm still sweating the next job, and probably always will.

The *Indianapolis* project has to do with the navy cruiser that was supposed to meet up with the U.S. fleet in the Philippines after it delivered atomic bomb parts to the Marianas. Well, it was struck by two torpedoes from a Japanese sub and sank within twelve minutes. There were twelve hundred guys on board; eight hundred went into the water; they didn't have time to get the lifeboats out. The first day they said, "Don't worry, the navy's going to come." By the second day, the sharks came. By the third day they were going crazy, and by the fourth day they were killing each other. The navy had lost track of the ship. It was unaware the ship had sunk.

Now, embarrassed at this terrible tragedy—the worst sinking of the war in terms of lives lost—happening right at the end of the war, at the point the navy was about to crow about its victory in the Pacific, they decided to hang the blame on the captain of the ship. There was a kangaroo court-martial and the navy even brought over the skipper of the Japanese submarine to testify against the captain. Then the navy said to the sailors, most of them eighteen-year-old kids, "Forget about all this, put it behind you, the war's over, go home, get married, get a job, be happy." And that's what they all tried to do. They came home and married the girls next door and started their lives and had their kids and none of them talked about it, not to anyone; they all kept it inside. Then, in 1968, the captain walked down the front steps of his house in Connecticut and blew his head off.

Around that time the crew started having reunions. There were twenty guys at first, then forty, then eighty. And the more they got together, the more they realized they all had had the same experience. None of them could sleep, none of them had put the experience behind them. And each one had thought on his own that there was something wrong with him. So they decided that what they wanted to do to make themselves whole was to exonerate the captain whom they loved. And they did it— they got a Senate resolution saying the navy was wrong, and the ship got a Presidential Unit Citation.

Anyway, so a guy comes to me and pitches me the

story—asks if I want to write the screenplay. And at first I said, "Which story do you do? There are three stories. There's a ship sinking and guys surviving. There's the court-martial story, and then there's old guys going to Congress and trying to get redress from the government."

I said, "Okay, here's what I'm going to do. I'm going to go interview a bunch of the survivors and think about the script. You pay me for my time and I'll come back and tell you if I can do it or not. If I say no, then you're entitled to all my research. I don't want to take this on until I know I can do it, until I have a way to do it." I knew it was going to be a big project, and I didn't want to spend a year trying to do something I couldn't deliver. So I met the guys, and after awhile I realized how the story should be told, at least for me. I invented a seventeen-year-old sailor who sails on the ship in July 1945, and I tell the story from his point of view, all the way up to the present, when he's in his seventies. I think it's a great story, and I'm very grateful and pleased I figured out a way to tell it.

I think writers have inner motors that propel them through material. Maybe somebody sees the motor and maybe somebody doesn't. It almost doesn't matter. My motor on this one is really the idea that American men have changed drastically in the last fifty years. Those guys grew up in a world of stoicism, when John Wayne was the paradigm. They'd all been through the Depression, and everybody had hard World War stories to tell. You were no different than anybody else. On every street in the country there was a star in the window because some kid had died. What's changed over the years is that it's now seen as the right thing to say that the government fucked you, instead of just swallowing it and saying it could have been worse. That's a great engine to get passionate about.

I met Alan Ball in his Hollywood office, the day after HBO ordered thirteen episodes of his new series, *Six Feet Under,* about a dysfunctional family of morticians. We began the conversation by talking about how the Oscar for *American Beauty,* won just six months before, had changed his life.

I'M NOW IN THE POSITION WHERE A LOT OF IMPORTANT people are coming to me and asking me to write scripts. It's weird, because *American Beauty* was something that I just wrote on my own for myself, and it brought me the most success I've ever had in my life. The lesson I learned from that was that I do better work when I write the movie that I would like to go see, as opposed to writing the movie that someone else would like me to write. Usually when you're a screenwriter in this town, you're a hired gun, writing someone else's vision; and there's a dilution that takes place in that transaction. I've been pitched so many stories and have read so many scripts that

people want me to write or rewrite, and I'm just not interested now. It's rare to meet someone who has a story
or an idea that sparks me. Tom Hanks pitched a story
that really did, so I'm writing it. It's about a cop in a
1960s rustbelt urban city that's in the throes of decay, and
he's investigating the murder of someone he loves. It's very
character-driven. I wouldn't call it a comedy. I see it as a
drama. But it's hard for me to write stuff that doesn't have
some humor in it, because I just get bored unless there's
something funny in it. If you're writing something that's
very dramatic, you're going to look for comedic moments
that lighten the tension. Anyway, I don't think in terms
of comedy or drama. I think in terms of what works.

There were moments in *American Beauty* where audi-
ences were laughing at something just moments after being
moved by something else. That's a tone that I really respond to and that I like, because it's closest to the way I
see the world. It's not that I see things in terms of dark
irony, necessarily. I just see a darkness in the world. I
remember reading a book about acting called *Audition*,
which talks about the twelve certain things that make up
a good audition—and therefore good acting. One of them
is humor. The author, Michael Shurtleff, describes humor
as that way of seeing the world that keeps us from throw-
ing ourselves off a cliff. That resonates with me. I've always enjoyed laughing, making people laugh. As a kid, I
was a cutup—the class clown and then the class smart-
ass. I grew up in Marietta, Georgia—Newt Gingrich's
congressional district and home of the big chicken; there's
a big Kentucky Fried Chicken with a sixty-foot-high

chicken head. It's a very repressed place. A hotbed of narrow-mindedness. I just always knew that there was something else lurking beneath all that advertised piety. Which is *American Beauty*.

My first exposure to the arts was movies on television. I remember being totally entranced by all those film versions of Tennessee Williams plays—those great, lurid melodramas of the late fifties and early sixties: *Cat on a Hot Tin Roof, Summer and Smoke, A Streetcar Named Desire*. They were all so Gothic and twisted and weird and Southern, and I could identify with a lot of aspects of those plays; I just loved them. It never crossed my mind to try to become a filmmaker, to try to become involved in the film industry, other than by being an actor. When I went to college it was to become an actor. But I had already written plays, for me and my friends in high school. In the first grade I wrote a play about the Easter bunny, and we performed it for the PTA. All I remember is that I cast myself in it, playing the Easter bunny, and there was a big egg fight at the end. It just never crossed my mind to pursue filmmaking; I wasn't around it, I wasn't close to it.

It was relatively recently that I began making a living as a writer. I had a day job, working as a graphic designer at *Adweek* magazine, and I was a resident playwright for a New York theater company, Alarm Dog Rep. I doubt you've heard of it. Writing wasn't my job, it was a labor of love, and because I was producing my own work, I never had to deal with the politics. My day job paid my bills, and I got used to writing just for the love of it. I never wrote something and thought, "Well I need to do this to make this sell." I wrote what I thought would be fun or interesting or exciting.

One of my plays is called *Five Women Wearing the Same Dress.* David Tochterman, a talent scout for Carsey-Werner Television, saw it and asked to meet with me. That was in 1992. He spent the whole meeting telling me why I should vote for Ross Perot, and I walked away thinking, "Well, *that* was surreal." A year or so later I got a job offer to come out and write for the second season of *Grace Under Fire.* My theater company had sort of fallen apart and I was sick of living in New York and was ready for a big change in life and I figured what the hell.

When I got the job offer, I'd never even seen the show; I didn't watch much TV at all. But I came out and spent a year on the show and was very lucky. Working on *Grace* and then *Cybill,* I worked for shows on which the stars had creative control, and they would have these meltdowns in the middle of the season and fire half the staff, and those of us who stuck around got big promotions. I climbed the ranks pretty fast, and that's the only reason why. I stuck around. Everybody else would get fired.

Prior to this, my two screenwriting experiences had both been fairly typical development hells. I'd been hired by Columbia to adapt my play, and I'd also done an assignment rewrite for Warner Bros. The Columbia gig was especially weird. I'd had no experience working with people from film or TV, and when they flew me first-class to Los Angeles I sat next to Richard Gere. It was all very glamorous and I was completely intimidated by it. I met with executives at the studio and they gave me all their notes, and as is usual in the case of development, all the notes conflicted with one another and were sort of random, and I took all of them because I just assumed that's what you did. I'm sure they thought they were making the movie better, but as those notes tend to be, they were fairly recycled. It was like, "Oh, couldn't we have a moment like that other movie when . . . ," and "Wouldn't it be great to have a flashback to when these characters were kids?"

It makes my skin crawl to look at that script now, because it's really bad, but it was the first time I was being paid to do something like that, so I thought that's what you did. And at that point in my career I was in no position to say, "You know, I don't think that's such a good idea" and walk away from it. I needed the work. Same with the thing I did for Warner Bros. In both those instances I was trying to write what I thought they wanted, trying to give them my version of a Hollywood movie with roles that would appeal to movie stars and that had a happy ending. That's just not who I am. And the results were not successful—which is why those scripts haven't been made.

I hope they won't be, either, as sometimes happens when writers win Oscars or other awards. People often ask about *Five Women Wearing the Same Dress*. I hear every now and then that there's some interest or someone read it and thought it was good. We actually had a reading of it at my agency last summer with movie stars who sat around the table and read parts, and everybody said,

"Omigod, it's so good," and I thought, No it isn't; it's not particularly good. Just because I wrote this other movie that turned out to be good doesn't mean this is good.

But then, a lot of people don't know what's good. A lot of people in very high places do not know what is good and cannot tell good from bad or mediocre. I think by my own standards now, that script I wrote isn't good and I don't want it produced, even though it's better, probably, than a lot of what gets produced these days. But I don't want to go back and revisit those characters and that script, because I've moved on. And I don't really feel like it's the kind of movie I want to do. It's a little pat. It's a little easy.

A large percentage of what the entertainment industry creates is without substance, and a lot of that is the feel-good stuff. Hey, I love to lie on my couch at home and watch those movies on satellite, but I don't want to make them. I'd rather work on something that gets me involved and passionate. Years from now when I've run out of whatever cachet—and cash—I have I'm sure I'll be happy to write *Police Academy 12*.

One of the great things about working in TV was learning to be much more disciplined about writing than I had been before; you gotta be there, you gotta do it, you gotta stay there till it's done. Deadlines are good for me, so even if I don't have one, I'll impose one, as I did with *American Beauty*.

For two years I worked on *Cybill* and really hated it, and then I went back for a third year because they threw so much money at me. I felt like such a whore. It was really the first time in my life that I did something just for the money, and I felt bad about it. I really did. I was doing work that I really didn't care about. In order to get through the week, I had to put aside any passion I might feel about the writing. I became a craftsman, knowing that they wanted a moment when the star instructs them all about something, then a big laugh here, then for somebody to hug and learn a lesson and some sappy music and a big joke that we'll give to her because she's the star, and then we'll cut. There was a very specific formula that you had to use to make everyone happy. I thought what we were putting on the air was pretty awful, and I was becoming in a lot of ways like Lester, in *American Beauty*— a man who'd lost his passion for life. I had lost my passion for writing, which had been for a long time a cornerstone of my existence.

The only way I could justify doing that was by convincing myself that I was buying the freedom to write what I wanted to write, something I could care about and feel passionate about; something that was about something, rather than about people in designer clothing trading insults between advertisements. I promised myself that I would have *American Beauty* finished by the time I finished that final season. And I did.

The impetus for the script had come about ten years before, when I was living in New York. Walking home from lunch one Sunday, I had an encounter in front of the World Trade Center. The encounter was with a plastic bag that just blew out of nowhere and circled me twenty times. It was weirdly spiritual. I just stopped and let it do that.

I know this sounds kind of flaky, but I knew that I was in the presence of something. And I never forgot that moment. Later, during the Amy Fisher–Joey Buttafuoco trial, I remember thinking that this whole episode was being played out publicly in a kind of dramatic, tabloid entertainment way that we're all sort of fascinated by, but I knew that underneath this spectacle there was something real that had happened, and real lives were going terribly astray; a real tragedy had happened that became a national joke. I knew that there was a truth underneath it all that was more interesting and more textured than anything on the news and in the tabloids and in those made-for-TV movies, and that the truth was something we were never going to know and that would be known only by the participants. I found that very fascinating.

The script was originally built around a big media trial where the videotape you see at the beginning of the movie had found its way into the hands of the police, and the kids were on trial. The scene ended up being cut out of the film, but that was the context in which I wrote it.

I started writing it as a play while still living in New York City. I got about forty-five pages into the play, and it just didn't work; it was too wordy, given how visual the story was. I had this big blank screen upstage where you would see Ricky's videotapes, and it was weird. I just dropped it. Years later, I picked it up again, specifically as a screenplay, because my new agent, Andrew Cannava, had told me I needed to write a new script, and then I dropped it again until I imposed that deadline.

Returning to *American Beauty* after four years of writing episodic television, I rediscovered my passion for writing the same way Lester rediscovers his passion for life. What I learned is that you should write what you care about—write what moves you; write what intrigues you and you find compelling; write what angers you and makes you sad.

The most interesting thing for me as a writer is and always has been character: people whose lives are complicated; people who are struggling to make the right choice in a morally ambiguous universe; people who are striving to live authentic lives in a world that is increasingly inauthentic. I think in terms of characters that I just happen to stumble upon and am fascinated by. They're so much more interesting to me than any one-note high-concept pitch. The best work that I do is hard to encapsulate in one sentence. It's more complex than that. I'm more interested in the guy who keeps acting in ways that are antithetical to his best interests but he just can't see it. Of course, you start talking like this to executives and their eyes glaze over. On the other hand, if someone came to me with a pitch, "He used to be married to her, and she died and came back as a dog, and he gets her at the pound!" And I'm like, Yeah, so. My eyes glaze over at *that* stuff.

Before I actually begin writing, I'll do a lot of preliminary thinking and outlining, but only on a barely conscious level. I have tons of files on my computer that are just random thoughts. Only occasionally do I look back at them. It seems that just the act of writing them down cements them in my head; I rarely forget them. By the time

I sit down at the keyboard and begin typing, my characters have really sort of revealed themselves to me. I'm aware of who they are, and I'm in their skin in the sense that their dilemmas are very compelling to me. I may not know how old they are, exactly, or what they do for a living, but there's a core of who they are.

Writing teaches me what I believe, what my values are. It's actually sort of terrifying. Watching *American Beauty* with an audience for the first time was really terrifying, because it was like, "Okay, there's my subconscious up there on this big screen. What do you think?" I wanted to run and hide; it was all too personal. But if you're driven to write, on some level you have a need or a desire to share yourself with the world. Even as a kid I wrote little comic books and stories. I had these action figures and I'd create entire neighborhoods with toy cars and houses and little army men and families with intricate relationships—and then they'd always all get wiped out by an earthquake or some other natural disaster. Everybody always died. I don't know why. Maybe it had something to do with coming along late in my own family, many years after my brothers. By then, my parents were pretty much exhausted from raising kids, so I was kind of left to my own devices. I developed a very active imagination, just to keep myself entertained.

I suppose that, in a sense, writing is a form of therapy. It's a discovery process. Human behavior fascinates me. I think I have a pretty good understanding of psychology, but I never analyze my characters; they seem like real people to me, which I'm sure is some form of madness. It's either sitting here and writing or sitting on the subway and talking to myself. That runs contrary to the industry, which wants to pinpoint a formula—take a more scientific approach to things. I can't do that. Deconstructing the process bores me; my brain shuts down. I don't believe there is a given formula, a key to success. There's an element of luck and synchronicity that happens sometimes, and you can't make it happen; you can't force it to happen. I mean, how many movies have you seen in which the right elements have been in place and something just didn't click, it didn't work?

I know that some people think *American Beauty* is cynical. Maybe on the surface it is. But underneath the cynicism is a real romanticism. If a person really wakes up one day and is filled with excitement and optimism and for whatever reason rediscovers his purpose in life and then walks out the front door and gets hit by a bus, is that cynical? I don't think so. At least he was fully alive when it happened. So Lester's being murdered at the end doesn't make the movie cynical. The story takes place in a cynical world and is about a cynical man who rediscovers his noncynical self, in the most surprising way. He's not fully alive until he makes someone more important than himself. And that happens when he finds himself in the presence of something larger than he is, which is his concern for the well-being of this young girl.

We live in a culture that has a lot of false gods and that tends to promote a system of values that, I think, runs counter to what we as human beings need and are capable of. It's all in the service and pursuit of money—the notion that stuff can make your life better. I love that scene in *American Beauty* when Lester says, "This isn't life, this is just stuff."

Are there hard and fast screenwriting rules? Yeah, you have to be interested in the story you're writing. Any other rule I can't articulate, because the rest are all intuitive. I follow my instincts. At an American Film Institute seminar someone said that I'd broken a lot of rules in the *American Beauty* screenplay. I said, "I don't know what those rules were." And I don't. I didn't consciously break rules. I just wrote the story in a way that interested me.

People said to me, "That's so inventive and unusual that you had a dead man narrate a film." Turns out that a lot of people, even in Hollywood, haven't seen *Sunset Boulevard,* which is narrated by a dead man and came out fifty years ago.

Other people said, "What about all that narration at the beginning? You're not supposed to have narration." I said, "When was that decided?" I guess there must have been a lot of bad narration in a lot of bad movies. It's sort of that whole Hollywood way of thinking, that this $90 million movie will come out that's terrible about earthquakes and no one goes to see it because it's so horrible, then the conventional wisdom is that no one wants to see movies about earthquakes. They don't say, "I guess no one wants to see movies that are bad and bloated and rewritten by seventy different people; movies that have overdosed on committee thinking because the budget was so expensive to make that every person in the studio had to put in their two cents." Instead, they say that no one wants to see earthquake movies. Look at *Rocky*. The conventional wisdom in the mid-seventies was that no one liked boxing movies. Then *Rocky* came out and everybody went, so all of a sudden they thought people liked boxing movies—until people stopped going to see bad boxing movies. The truth is that people like movies if they're good.

As a writer, I'm only disciplined in a kind of sporadic way. I'll slough off for months and then all of a sudden I'll think that I have to get finished by a certain date—a deadline. It's really hard but I'll force myself. I don't know if other writers experience this, but when I sit down in front of the computer, all of a sudden cleaning the refrigerator becomes incredibly attractive. I think, "You know what? I really should reorganize my files. I haven't done that for a while." It's just a trap. It's avoidance. I don't know why something that I love as much as I love writing, something that provides my life with so much meaning, and pays my bills, why it's such a chore, and why I would avoid it as much as I do. It's hard work.

And yet there are times when I just lose myself in it, moments when it's as if the script takes on its own life and I'm surprised by what's going on. There is a certain kind of zone that I chance upon sometimes. It's a place in which that layer between the conscious and subconscious sort of opens for a moment. In a way, it's like channeling; you're not really thinking about it; there's a flow happening and you're a part of it, a witness. I don't think it's metaphysical, but there is a discipline involved in getting to that stage. I'm not really aware of how to help it along, so all I do is basically try not to get in its way. I tend to work better late at night; I'm just nocturnal that way. There's something about the dark.

But a lot of times I find that, even though I do work more at night, if the first thing I do in the morning is go sit down at the computer, I tend to be in a more receptive frame of mind. I think the zone, or whatever you want to call it, is almost like a dream state—not a trance, an alpha state. It's more intuitive and less structured. And I can't have any real contact with the real world, because that'll break the zone entirely. There are times when I have an entire day planned and I'll start writing and this door will open and things will flow and then I'll end up not leaving my house that day. I'll sit there and the next thing I know, it's six o'clock and I haven't eaten all day. Even if I feel hungry, a part of me thinks, "Don't go make a sandwich, because you may lose this. The refrigerator's always there." And there are times, rare, when I end up pounding out stuff for ten hours. It's not always good stuff, because sometimes you hit that vein of inspiration and go back and read it, and you wonder, "What was I thinking?"

I know that some writers say there's no correlation between how you think the work is going and how it's really going, but I usually tend to have a sense of when it's working dramatically: if I'm intrigued with what's going on between the characters or in the characters' lives. For instance, there's a moment in *American Beauty* when Carolyn tries to sell a house, and she's really bad at it and doesn't sell it, and when everyone leaves she locks herself in a room and starts slapping herself. I did not intend for that to happen; I was in one of those zone moments with things flowing, and when she started slapping herself and calling herself "Weak, baby," I was kind of appalled, thinking that this character is way more pathetic than I'd ever imagined; she's really tragic. It surprised me totally, but I knew that it was a very compelling moment, a moment that worked. You have to allow yourself as a writer to have your characters show more facets than you thought they had.

What separates the screenplay format from plays or even television is that movies really can tell a story visually; the movie becomes even more dreamlike than a play or four-camera television, which are both language-driven. I remember typing out some dialogue for *American Beauty* and getting to the point when Ricky says, "Do you want to see the most beautiful thing I've ever filmed?" and she says, "Sure," and I had to wonder then what it was, and I thought to myself what the most beautiful thing I ever saw was, and I immediately remembered that moment with the plastic bag back in New York. I'd never consciously thought to myself that I'd put it in a script one day; I just got to that point in the script and had to come up with the most beautiful thing, the thing that moved him most. What did I have to draw on? Well, it was that moment. I needed something real. Luckily, the movie was made by people who understood that image and envisioned what it could be and went with it, but it could very easily have been made by people who said, "Oh, come on, now! A plastic bag? Garbage?"

I spent the first part of my professional life pursuing

acting, and so I tend to play all the roles in my head as I write, and part of my process is going back and taking out all of the stage directions that refer to my own personal performance choices—that is, all the stuff that doesn't make any sense in terms of propelling the story or providing information. I get into a zone and write dialogue and say, "She sighs and stares at the floor." In my head, that's what I'm doing when I'm playing that role. And then I realize that that doesn't say anything. So I have to figure out another way to say it in a way that's necessary for the read and is also necessary to convey the emotional state of the character without its being vague and performance-oriented.

My years as an actor have a lot to do with my being a writer now. It's as if I can channel my characters the same way actors do; I'm aware of what upsets them, for instance, and a lot of times it's not what upsets me.

I certainly didn't plan things this way, but I guess my whole life has been pointed toward my being a screenwriter. The lies and stories I told as a kid; being a graphic artist and understanding visuals; being an actor and knowing what actors like; being a playwright and learning what dialogue can and can't do. It's the perfect screenwriter's résumé.

Some people are surprised that I'm not concentrating only on movies. But HBO is really behind this series. And also, I got to direct the pilot, which is something I've wanted to do. It's part of my master plan; I eventually want to write and direct. Directing an hour pilot as a rookie is a lot less intimidating than directing a two-hour feature. Prior to selling the script for *American Beauty*, I'd signed a television development deal and did a sitcom for ABC, which got canceled. That was really an awful experience. It was called *Oh Grow Up*. No one ever knew it was on the air. It was the worst of dealing with networks and their notes and their not believing in the show and expecting you to be a hit out of the gate and if you're not they bail on you immediately, and also all the weird politics. Anyway, I had eighteen months left on my TV deal, so I was required to do another pilot, and I just did not want to do another show for the networks, because it's just so creatively infuriating and stultifying, and I really truly believe that network television is a marketing medium before anything else, and that programming is really filler between commercials. They say they want something new and original and edgy, and then you give them that and the first thing they do is iron all the interesting and edgy and original material out of it. If you watch network TV you'll notice that, on a purely kinetic level, the most interesting stuff are the advertisements. That's why it exists, to sell products, and that totally impacts the work that you do on a series. I could not go back into that arena; I would've had to blow my brains out. So I wrote this pilot on spec, knowing that the only place that would produce it would be cable, and it satisfied my obligation to my contract. It's turned out to be win-win.

I must be the luckiest guy in Hollywood, because my experience with HBO is remarkably similar to my experience with DreamWorks on *American Beauty*. Both seem to really respond to the material and believe it has a unique, specific voice, and neither wants to mess with that. Of course, I didn't direct *American Beauty,* so I'm sure Sam Mendes got a lot more notes than I did, because people tend to assume that the director of a movie is its author, which is a notion I have just a little bit of a problem with. When a film begins "A Film by," something in me bristles. Studios, for the most part, tend to view writers as expendable and the director as the main creative force— which is certainly the case many times.

Writers aren't generally held in high esteem in Hollywood. The reason, I think, is that a lot of people who green-light movies and call the shots are not very creative. Most development people at the studios tend to think in terms of things that have been proven; they like moments that have already played in other movies. They can't read a script and see the potential for what it can be. Probably, a lot of people in those positions are not really qualified to be in those positions. (But in that regard movie-making is no different from any other industry.) My experiences in "development" have been baffling to me. Also, it's just the hierarchy of the studios. You will work with these lower-level people on a rewrite and give them your version, and then they'll give your script to the upper-level people to read, and it's like they've never had a conversation. How many scripts a day do they read? They read a script once on the Stairmaster at the gym, and they make some sweeping judgment about it: "I don't know, I just didn't care about the whole lawyer aspect of it. Can't they be doctors?" And because of their position at the studio you take it back to the writer with a note to make them doctors. The executives don't know how to read a script and lose themselves in it and see the world that it conveys. Which is why so much is homogenized and formulaic, and style and not substance. They follow all the rules but don't really go anywhere.

But that's an aside. It wasn't true on *American Beauty*. I was very fortunate to work with a brilliant director who liked and responded to the script. A lot of directors will read a script and say, "Oh, that reminds me of this other story, so let's make a movie about that." And then you hire someone to rewrite that script, and by then the power structure at the studio has changed, so that movie doesn't get green-lit there and has to go somewhere else, and the new executive has another idea, so what finally gets on the screen has been translated and interpreted by fourteen different people. And you can tell. It's just a mess.

Most likely, *American Beauty* will be a once-in-a-lifetime experience. It's somewhat of a Cinderella story. I'm one of the luckiest men in the history of the entertainment industry. I wrote this script, it was made pretty much intact, made exactly the way it needed to be and marketed the right way, and for whatever reason it hit a nerve at this specific point in time. The rest is history.

Projects take on their own lives. They assume their own energy, and part of what you have to do is recognize when that's happening and get out of its way. That happens for me as a writer, too. I can't say that I control my process, and if I ever try to control it too much, I lose it all. I mean, you can be disciplined; you can make sure that you practice your craft daily by sitting there and by working, but in terms of refining it into some easily articulated technique or formula, no. There's an element of mystery that I appreciate and would hate to lose.

When you talk to Stephen Gaghan, you learn that sometimes the story is about screenwriting, and sometimes it's about the screenwriter. He was only thirty-five when we spoke (and had just won the Oscar for *Traffic*), but his biography of despair and adventure and surprise left me breathless—and in some ways reminded me of Jack London's journeys on his way to becoming a writer. I began the interview, innocently enough, by asking what made him want to write in the first place.

I THINK YOU'LL HAVE TO BLAME READING FOR MY BEcoming a writer. I grew up in Louisville, Kentucky, and used to walk to the Frankfort Avenue branch of the public library, near my house, and walk out with eight or ten books under my arm. People would walk by me and say, "Oh, what a little bookworm." Writers became my heroes. I looked up to them—Hemingway and Fitzgerald, Faulkner and Joyce. All I have to do is look at the copy of *Go Down, Moses* on my nightstand and I feel happy just knowing that Faulkner wrote *The Bear*.

Writing was definitely in my family. My grandfather was a journalist who had a drinking problem. He used to carry a card in his wallet that said, "If you find me, call my son"—my dad—at such and such a number. At seven years old I told my mom I wanted to be a writer, and she said, "Oh, honey, you'll live in misery and go, and by go, I mean die, teaching other people's children badly." That must've stuck pretty well in my head, because I tried to do a lot of other things first before I became a writer. I didn't want to be indigent, and writing didn't seem like a realistic way to make a living. Except for my grandfather, I didn't know anyone who made a living as a writer, so I always had the feeling that I should do something else— something that could provide a small annuity and keep me writing on the side; then (when my ship came in) I'd write full-time. I remember hearing that one time when Preston Sturges was broke, he joked that the Nietzschean cant of "live dangerously" should be rewritten to say, "Live dangerously on a small income."

My dad, who was a real character, got cancer and was sick for a long time. It's very strange and very hard to see someone you love die slowly in your study. I responded in the old-fashioned way—by anesthetizing myself for a couple of years. The night before his funeral I broke into the pills—Librium, morphine, whatever was around—and washed them down with some Jack Daniel's. The next morning, I threw up on the way to the funeral. Everyone thought it was grief, which it was. I pretty much stayed stoned, on pot and pills and booze, for the next couple of years. You know, Kentucky is a place where everybody drinks alcohol and everybody smokes cigarettes. It's a matter of civic pride to support the local industries. The Maker's Mark bourbon distillery is about a forty-five-minute drive. I can remember mixing up Vodka Collinses in fast-food cups and taking them to school with me. They would say Burger King on the outside, but there would be a Vodka Collins inside.

I got kicked out of high school on the last day of my senior year for driving a go-cart through the administration building. Before then, and for a pretty long time, I'd been at the top of my class—a National Merit scholar, all-state in soccer and captain of the team, and captain of the tennis team—that kind of crap. And I'd done a lot of stuff to build my résumé for Ivy League schools. You know: "Be a thespian, because it will get you into Yale." "Be president of Spanish Club, because it will get you into Harvard." Nothing seemed to be done for anything other than résumé building. Nothing was for the joy of it. Everything I did was to build myself into some perfect young Renaissance duke, in order to get into the ruling class where I would rule with a well-tempered hand. And at some point, that stopped working for me.

When you're young, it's really easy to be a winner. You win and you think, "I'm winning and now everything is just perfect. Look, everything is the way it's supposed to be." For me, just the process of going into high school started changing things; I wasn't winning in the way I wanted to, even though it probably appeared to outsiders that I was still winning. I think what happened is that, in some ways, I just quit. I said, "Well, if it's not going to work, I don't want to do it." Essentially, I ran away; I got drunk and ran away. It was the soccer-tennis conundrum. When I played soccer, I'd say I was a tennis player, and when I played tennis, I'd say I was a soccer player.

Then I started focusing on what I liked to do, not what I thought I should do, and what I liked to do was drink and read books and chase girls. Life with only one of them didn't work too well. Life with two was fairly tolerable. But life with three was just absolutely perfect.

I did a lot of traveling and a lot of wandering around. I was drunk in a lot of cities, and got arrested for all sorts of things, like inciting a riot in Miami. I was seventeen.

At twenty-two I published a short story in *The Iowa Review,* which is pretty prestigious, but after that it got increasingly difficult to complete a short story, and the thought of actually writing a full novel was excruciating. At one point, when I was living in an abandoned farmhouse in New Hampshire, I realized I'd spent six weeks working on a single paragraph—and most of that time on just the first sentence.

I'd raised some money and started a catalog company called Fallen Empire that sold things—coats, bookshelves, basically anything we liked—a bunch of them from our own design. What made us different is that we were the first truly ironic catalog. We went out of business when J. Peterman sued me on a "look and feel" copyright violation. So there I was, in Federal Court in New York, with a $450 an hour lawyer. I think Peterman thought I was some big company backed by Land's End instead of a kid trying to sell bicycle-messenger bags. The judge was great.

He said, "I want you two guys"—Peterman and me—"to have lunch without your lawyers." So we did; we got some sandwiches and sat and talked for about twenty minutes and worked it all out. But by then it had cost me $60,000 in legal fees, and we were essentially out of business. So I decided to stay in New York and write full-time. Somehow I'd managed to get $280 a week on unemployment and figured I could make a go of it. I ended up getting a job at *The Paris Review,* which was a wonderful place to observe the literary life, if not to actively write.

It was in New York I discovered I have a talent for befriending bartenders. I found places where I could go and drink for free. If I hadn't done that, I wouldn't have been able to stay in New York, because I couldn't afford to drink in the style to which I'd become accustomed. Between the *Review* and my unemployment—for as long as it lasted—and some freelance copywriting, I could just eke out a living as a kind of a cut-rate Ginger Man—"God's mercy on the wild Ginger Man" as J. P. Donleavy put it. Obviously, fiction writing had fallen far into the background. It's exhausting trying to write a sentence when your primary activity is somehow coming up with the resources it takes to maintain a steady intake of substances, let alone the rent. I don't know how I did it. In some weird way, it's kind of heroic; I was a hero of my own epic. It's the "Song of Roland" redone as a "Song of Stephen." *Wakes up and must get high. How will it happen? He has no money and is months behind in rent. See him descend from his fifth-floor walk-up to the street with nary a plan. Maybe over to Plimpton's apartment to hang out for a little while. Drink some scotch from the pool room. Get a grip on the day. The young swain. Out in New York. Living the literary high life.*

Friends of mine were moving on with their lives. They had real jobs and were going out to summer places and paying the rent themselves, and I was going in the exact opposite direction.

Then something very strange happened—strange but true. I had an old television set that got only two stations through its aluminum-foil antenna, and the stations happened to be the ones that played *The Simpsons* and reruns of *Seinfeld*. So every night around seven-thirty, I'd watch them. Well, one night in August, when everyone's out in Amagansett and Sagaponack or wherever, and it's a hundred degrees with a hundred percent humidity, and I'm sitting in my living room, trying to figure out who I can call to borrow a six-pack and watching *The Simpsons,* I happen to look over and see this *New York Times* story about television writers who were so, so rich. And I think, "Fuck art. I want a sandwich." So I sat down and wrote an episode of *The Simpsons* in a day—eighty pages without even knowing what a real TV script looked like. That was so much fun, I decided to do a *Seinfeld*. So I did that, too, and at the end of three days I had these two scripts and thought it was really going well, especially considering I'd once taken six weeks to write a single sentence. I wanted to keep it going, and four days later I finished a screenplay called *The Underachievers,* about some people who tried to start a catalog company in Chicago. What a great week that was. I think what fueled it was the frustration of not having done anything for so long. If you're a writer, there is nothing worse than not writing. Not writing is a very unpleasant way to live. It's hell, actually.

I gave the scripts to a guy I know who worked in the mail room at InterTalent. He'd been a lawyer at a white-shoe firm in Boston where they handled Kennedy stuff, but he was interested in the entertainment business and wanted to be an agent, and that's where you start, in the mail room. What he did was give the scripts to one of the junior agents on Sam Simon's account, Sam being one of the original writers and executive producers on *The Simpsons,* so my *Simpsons* script found its way to Sam. It was eighty pages and a huge mess, but I heard he read it and said the writing was good and he'd hire somebody who wrote like that. When I got this feedback, I sent the other stuff to Bernie Brillstein—just mailed it to his office, out of the blue—because I'd heard about him with the *Saturday Night Live* guys. To tell you the truth, to this day I haven't the slightest idea how it happened, but Bernie Brillstein actually read the package. About a week after sending it out, I came home one night and there's a message from him, "If you ever get to L.A., call me." It was like getting a communication from an alien spaceship. I just walked around all day in a daze.

Then I went back to normal and sat with my other indigent friends in Central Park and watched people sail their little boats around the little duck pond and drank coffee and tried to decide how we were going to spend the rest of our day, which was usually by going downtown to try to score some drugs and drink some free drinks from one of the people we knew.

I decided the time had come to visit L.A. The scenario in my mind was clear. I'd show up and be hired right away on *The Simpsons*—but when I got there it turned out that Sam Simon had left and David Mirkin was the boss. Someone told me he said that my script was "not Simpsonsesque," and that was that. I ended up sleeping on my friend's floor in Koreatown for a couple of weeks, went back to New York for a while, then came out to L.A. right after Christmas and called Bernie Brillstein. He said he'd pay me $750 a week to answer phones for his development executive, though the job was really a kind of a junior development job, so to get it I had to audition by writing something called "coverage." I had to ask a friend what it was before writing it. Anyway, I got the job, which was great because not only did I get my salary, but they also paid me eighty bucks for each novel I read and wrote coverage on. In three weeks I read about twenty novels, all of my own choosing. I read all the Walker Percy novels to determine whether or not they would be good movies— and decided, of course, that every single one would be a great movie. I'd write these long, detailed documents about why *The Last Gentleman* would be the greatest movie ever. *Lancelot*. The greatest movie ever. Naturally, a great book doesn't necessarily make a great movie, so I was way off base, but at the end of a few weeks I'd saved about two grand—and quit. I just quit. I wasn't even there long enough to have my ideas rejected. But I could see there'd never be any time to write. They let me continue to cover novels for them while I wrote scripts at home.

The rejections piled up, hundreds of them. I'd write things and think something was going to happen, and it almost would. I *almost* got hired on sitcoms, and then I *almost* got hired here, *almost* got hired there, *almost* got hired everywhere. I remember pitching to *The Red Shoe Diaries,* the erotic series on Showtime, and sitting across from Zalman King's partner. He had my *Simpsons* script and my *Iowa Review* short story and my *Underachievers* screenplay, and he looked at them as if they were a pile of feces—which they were, except for the short story. He said, "You look like a clever boy, but what do you know about love?" And I said, "I don't know anything about love. But I know I can get Joan Severance naked inside of two minutes and the story will make sense." And he looked at me and let out this very slow laugh—"Ha . . . ha . . . ha." I also got rejected by *Baywatch Nights* over the telephone. Those are just a few examples. It happened hundreds of times. Believe me, if I'd had any idea how it worked, I would have quit, I'm sure. My best friend was ignorance. Don't underestimate its importance.

My office was this hundred-buck-a-month place on the fourth floor of a building on the corner of Hollywood and Cahuenga; it was actually a co-op of writers called—yes— the Fourth Floor. I took the bus there every day and wrote, and that's where I met Robert Ward, who'd been a writer on *Miami Vice* and *Hill Street Blues,* and he was also a novelist. I liked his first novel, *Shedding Skin.* Anyway, at some point, he was running the writing staff at *New York Undercover* for Dick Wolf and had a freelance script to give out, so he gave it to me and another writer named Michael Perry. We turned in our first draft, which we thought was great, and went in to see Bob. He almost couldn't convey his disappointment, so we went back to the drawing board and worked hard and turned out a pretty good script. And it got produced. That was a very big deal, because things started moving a lot faster.

I ended up getting hired by Robert Palm on staff for the first season of *American Gothic*. It was a wonderful show, beautifully written, with all these Southern literary qualities—right up my alley. I loved writing it, and helped write seven episodes that first season. Then I was hired by David E. Kelly for the first thirteen episodes of *The Practice*. That was sort of interesting—being rewritten to the level which he rewrites you. I knew that wasn't for me, so I left.

Anyway, while I was working on *The Practice,* David Milch gave me a freelance episode of *NYPD Blue,* which we shared an Emmy for. I think we won because of this incredible speech David wrote at the end of the script for this character who'd been a Vietnam vet; it was about his coming back to America and getting a job as an undercover guy, and he was trying to explain he'd become a racist because his dad had been blinded by a black guy with a ballpeen hammer when he was trying to read a gas meter in the projects. It was a beautiful soliloquy.

I remember when he wrote it. You could see it was the real thing. And he was high from it. That made a big impact on me, seeing someone who really had it. I'd already admired him from a distance, because I'd known of him in New York; I'd heard stories from people who knew him when he was at Yale. I mean it, some of David's writing on *NYPD Blue* is as good dramatically as you'll find anywhere at anytime—and I mean anywhere. You can look at Chekhov and Tennessee Williams and O'Neill and Arthur Miller's best plays, and you can look at Tom Stoppard and you can look at whoever you want; for a couple of episodes in that first season his writing was up there. And that's coming from someone who loathes television.

About the same time I collaborated with Michael Tolkin on a script called *Twenty Billion,* a satire about Bill Gates that so far hasn't been made, and I took from that experience the same sort of message. What I learned was that this was an art form, writing scripts; it wasn't hack work to be condescended to until my big literary career got rolling. It was real. I learned that a script could hold everything I could put in it.

So that's what started creeping into my brain, and pretty soon I knew that if I didn't want to be a joke, I'd have to untie my hands and my legs and give up this whole other lifestyle of addiction. I was miserable anyway, cut off from life, and shamed by the experience of working with David and Michael. They were just so much better— profoundly better—than I was, and I realized I was never going to be half as good unless I got clean. These guys were artists. They put art into this form—not for money or for any other reason than the fact that they were artists. They were living lives that I thought were interesting and exemplary in a number of ways, and I could relate to that. It wasn't the perfect suburban existence that just repulsed me as a child. It was something else. And it inspired me.

On the other side of that, here I was, still going off on six-week binges where I'd take a hit of something within thirty seconds of waking up in the morning—if I went to bed at all. In the background would be some assignment that I wasn't doing, and then, at the last possible moment before the deadline, I'd stop taking everything and be so filled with self-loathing I would write like a maniac for four or five days, nonstop, not sleeping. It was the exact same coin, just the other side, and somehow I'd be able to finish the assignment and keep my job. I hated myself and couldn't feel for anyone or anything. It wasn't about being high or having fun anymore; it was about death. I could've died a hundred times in those last months.

And then I hit a place of, as they say, incomprehensible demoralization. I knew that if I didn't stop drinking and doing drugs, I was going to die. I'd just come off a five-day period without sleep and hit a wall. I remember that Sunday morning, eleven o'clock, and I'm sitting dead-center in the middle of my bed, cross-legged, my dog at the foot of the bed looking at me, with five or six empty bottles of red wine around. It was impossible to come down; impossible to get the edge off. That's when I called a friend who'd once been there himself, and he said he could help. And he did.

I didn't get better right away, of course; it took a couple of years. I started doing things every single day to stay sober. Every day. Every day. Consistently. And slowly but surely my life changed.

What happened to my writing was interesting. I had to start writing in a different way, from a different place. That took lot of therapy and a lot of help from a lot of people.

One of the first things I did after getting clean was set up *Traffic* on a pitch as a satire on the drug wars, with Ed Zwick directing. But I had trouble. I got totally bogged down and couldn't get it done, probably because I was trying to write in this different way—without bingeing and generating all that weird self-loathing. Months were going by with nothing happening on paper. I read all these books and newspaper articles and traveled to Washington and talked to people at think tanks and at the Department of Defense—and I couldn't get it done.

Right about then, Steven Soderbergh showed up and asked me about another script I'd written called *Havoc,* which is about some messed-up teenagers in Pacific Palisades. We talked for a long time and he told me he had the rights to the miniseries *Traffik,* from England. I said, "I love what you're talking about and how you want to do this, but the only problem is, I'm already doing it. It's set up at Fox 2000. Laura Ziskin bought the pitch and I'm writing it for E. J. Zwick." But I started thinking that maybe we could all throw our cards together, so I called Ed and asked him if he might be interested in joining the two projects together, with him producing and Steven directing. He thought about it and said, "It's a hard decision, but I really like Steven's work, and I could do that."

So everyone went off to re-jigger all the deals, and I still couldn't get over my writer's block. This was an important project to me, and the fact that I couldn't get it done made me wonder whether I just didn't have it in me to write without bingeing. I was in this no-man's land. Months and months were going by, and still nothing. People told me to have faith. The "F" word. So I sat there and sat there and sat there and waited for something to come. The good thing was that it took forever to make Steven's deal, which gave me an opportunity. I figured that I couldn't very well write if I didn't know which director I was writing for, so while Steven went off to shoot *Erin Brockovich*, I went over to Paramount and pitched myself as the screenwriter on a project they already had going, *Rules of Engagement*.

What happened was, Jim Webb, who'd been secretary of the navy, had written an original script that was truly, truly terrible; I mean, he's not really a screenwriter, he's not actually even a writer. But the idea, the story, was basically good, and they needed a screenwriter to pull it out. Well, Michele Manning at Paramount knew me from *Twenty Billion* and thought I might be able to do it, so she brought me in to meet with William Friedkin, the director, and Dick Zanuck, the producer. We just talked and talked and talked, and they ended up liking me and gave me a chance. It was a completely freak thing. There was no real reason for them to hire me, just one of those coincidences. I didn't love Jim Webb's script and Billy didn't either.

I wrote my first draft and threw out most of what Webb had written. My script ran 154 pages of what I thought was complete genius; I hadn't had a day, not a minute, of writer's block. Just up at 5 A.M. writing happily until nine at night. Dick had said, "Kid, get your passport. We're going to Yemen," which is where the movie's set. I didn't even bring a notebook or pen to the script meeting. So I show up and Friedkin says in a very low voice, "Dick thinks we're on the twenty-yard line. I don't even think we've gotten on the field." And he starts tearing this thing apart. I turned beet red and wanted to quit in the first two minutes. He said, "You want to make a $7 million movie for Showtime, I'll make a $7 million movie for Showtime! I've done that! And I can do it again. Back me up here, Dick." And Zanuck's shaking his head. "But if you want to make a $60 million movie, you've got to have a god-damned protagonist and a goddamned antagonist. And when the goddamned antagonist goes down, the audience gets out of their seats and they cheer." And I started to listen: What is this thing, the antagonist? And I thought that even if he wasn't right, he sure had a definitive point of view, so I went back and threw out eighty percent of that draft and three weeks later had another draft that everyone seemed to like.

Anyway, *Rules* finished up right around the time that *Erin Brockovich* started shooting, but now everyone's deal was in place. Even better, a year had gone by. All this stuff had been stewing inside of me, and now I had some real sobriety under my belt. I sat up in the corner of my bedroom and wrote the first draft in seven weeks, then drove from Malibu to West Hollywood and dropped it on Steven Soderbergh's front porch. He called me, and in this very understated way he has, he said, "This is pretty good. I'm going to do it. We're going to do this."

I did a few rewrites, but there are a lot of scenes in the movie basically unchanged from the first draft. What changed most was the whole Mexican scenario. I think it was Benicio Del Toro who asked, "Why does this guy have to be a bad guy necessarily?" That was great input, because I think we found a much deeper sense of humanity in the film through him.

Because of all the characters and the overlapping storylines, and because Steven likes to credit the intelligence of the audience, we operated by the principle: "What's the least amount of information we could give them and still have them get it?" It's a wonderful way to work.

I remember having trouble initially with the storyline for Helena, the Catherine Zeta-Jones character, the socialite who discovers her husband is a drug dealer the day he's arrested. In the miniseries, her character was way too melodramatic; I hadn't been able to get in touch with it, which made starting the script impossible. Then one night I suddenly woke up with a voice in my head—the voice of her character. She was saying, "Duck salad? You never eat duck salad? Well, I know I don't but they say now there's two types of fat. And one of them is a good fat. Good fat? They say there's good fat now? If there's good fat then how can you believe anything you're told?" I could hear those voices and thought literally someone was talking in the room, so I just got up and wrote down what she said at the country club with her friend, and that became the first scene I wrote in the whole movie.

No kidding, sometimes I tear up when I think about what's happened to me in the last few years. I'm so grateful. I've found love, and had a child, and have another one on the way. And I've produced work that I'm proud of, not embarrassed by. It used to be hard to write. I'd put so much pressure on myself. I'd sit down and crush myself with pressure to do something good. Now I just write. If it's good, great. And if it's not, well, I can try again. It's no longer the be-all and end-all. It's a part of a life, my life, and I couldn't trade it with anyone.